Secret Redemption

SUSAN KIMMEL

Copyright © 2019 – Susan Kimmel

All rights reserved. No part of this book may be used or reproduced in any manner, stored in a retrieval system, or transmitted in any form or by any means-electronic, mechanical, photocopy, recording, scanning or any other-except in the case of brief quotations in printed reviews, without the prior written permission from the author.

Scotland Press
3583 Scotland Road
Building 70
Scotland, PA 17254

ISBN : 978-0-578-61472-4

"The ultimate secrets are forever hidden in the most unlikely places!"

Table of Contents

Molly..1

Max...6

Max...10

Molly..12

Molly..20

Max...24

Molly..30

Max...35

Sheriff baxter 41

Molly..48

Max...57

Molly 60

Molly..66

Max...69

Molly..75

Max...83

Max...90

Sheriff baxter 97

Molly 101
Molly 105
Max 109
Max and molly 113
Molly 121
Molly 127
Max 133
Max 149
Max 151
John doe 155
Molly 163
Max and molly 166
Silas 169
Max 173
Sheriff baxter 181
Sheriff baxter 185
The trial 189
Family 192
Max and molly 195
Family 200

Chapter 1

MOLLY

Shadows of power lines hovered over the gray cemetery markers casting yet another layer of darkness to the already dreary countryside. Fresh tracks in the snow showed signs of a recent visitor.

Molly pulled back on the throttle, slowing the snowmobile until it came to a smooth stop. She hopped down from her seat and followed the footprints that led to a small stone marker with the name of John Doe. Kicking some of the snow away, she realized it was a newly dug grave. This must be the man she had heard about on the news. The report stated he had been a burn victim, denying fingerprints as identification. The local news station had produced a nation-wide search, but no one claimed to know him. With no family to pay for burial expenses, the county had laid him to rest by digging him a grave in the Chatham County Cemetery, located across the river from Pigeon Forge. The inhabitants of this 200-plot graveyard had been resting peacefully for over two centuries and with no living relatives to be remembered by, it was forgotten property in the town of Willow Grove.

Molly visited the cemetery often, not only on her snowmobile, but in the summer she rode her bicycle on the paths winding around the headstones, stopping occasionally to read the epitaphs and let her mind wonder about the families that lie beneath the ground. She had never encountered another living person in the cemetery and so the fresh tracks in the snow today caused her concern.

Knowing no one could hear her, Molly spoke out loud, tossing sarcasm into her voice. "Thank you, people of Willow Grove for the compassion you have shown this poor soul. He now lies here in a deserted graveyard, never to be grieved for, only to be forgotten. She said a small prayer, asking God to have mercy on him, no matter his story.

She bent down to investigate the fresh tracks, trying to decide if the footprints belonged to a man or a woman. If it was a woman, she had rather large feet, but the spacing of the steps made her sure it was a female. She saw something shining in the snow and bent over to pick it up. It was a small pendant in the shape of a hand, suspended from a silver chain. She had seen this same symbol often during her tour in Afghanistan. She had not been interested in the meaning then, but now it piqued her curiosity. Stopping by the library on the way home should give her an answer.

Her mind raced with many possibilities about the visitor. Was it his wife, or a sister? Maybe his mother. Speaking out loud again, Molly's strangely calm voice contradicted the anger flashing in her eyes. She couldn't understand how a man could be born, endure life, survive fire, possibly war, walk into a town and for unknown reasons, drop over dead with no one in the world recognizing him.

Molly's thoughts plunged into a maelstrom of emotion. She blinked back the moisture in her eyes as an odd sense of uneasiness tingled at the base of her spine. She gulped in a fresh breath of air, wondering where all these thoughts and feelings were coming from. Why was she suddenly feeling so uncomfortable? She had stopped at many gravesites, in the past years, to read epitaphs and she had never had these feelings before. She was feeling nauseated. She had witnessed many deaths in Afghanistan, but this was different. Why? Was John Doe someone she knew from her past? Her sixth sense whispered caution as she stood among the tombstones, pondering these questions.

For the first time since she had been coming to the cemetery, her awareness of the surroundings caught her off-guard. The crooked headstones scattered among the tangled weeds still looked proud, keeping to their duty, even as time had tried to wear away the messages they displayed.

The mysterious John Doe's final resting place, even though covered in snow, displayed no fancy statues of praying children or winged angels standing guard over his soul. In time, the small stone would shed chalky dust from softened broken edges, and dead leaves would gather in the corners, ignoring its existence. No one's memories deserved such action.

For some unexplainable reason Molly had been enticed by the mysterious footprints in the snow, leading to the pathetic marker. The line on the small stone between John Doe's date of birth and date of death was such a tiny mark, yet the dash represented his entire life. Who was he, and where was his family? Someone visited his grave. Someone who obviously missed him. Someone had let him die alone. But why? Why hadn't they claimed his body and given him a proper burial?

Molly sprang back onto the snowmobile, turned it toward the library, where she found information on the small hand shaped pendant, and then returned home.

John Doe would not leave Molly's thoughts. She wondered what kind of work he had done and where he was from. She visited the police department, to ask questions but they seemed to have no answers and they also seemed to have no interest in digging deeper into the case.

Molly was a registered nurse at the Willow Grove Medical Center, so she had some access to certain records. Finding the date of death for John Doe would be easy if she logged into the morgue. After that, she wasn't sure about her detective skills. She wasn't even sure she wanted to pursue this mission. She had dealt with death too often while serving in the Army and had been working hard at putting all that behind her. But maybe that was the reason she wanted to help John Doe. Whether he had been a soldier or civilian didn't matter. Either way, death had not been kind to him, a burn victim. Excruciating pain stalks the patient and changes him for life. According to the local paper, John Doe had burns over two-thirds of his body; more than many people could endure, especially with no family or friends to support him. And why was he alone? She wondered where he had come from and why had he come to Willow Grove?

As she drove to work a plan formed in her mind as to how she would help find John Doe's family and let them have some closure.

Molly wasn't one for calling in favors but as a nurse in Afghanistan, she had many GI's promise her the world if she could just take away their pain. Occasionally, she had sat by the bedside of a high-ranking officer, in charge of his recovery. She found them to be no more demanding than enlisted men. They just wanted someone to take care of them. She also never planned to get delivery on the pledges they had made to her in exchange for her overflow of compassion and skills. She had forgotten most of their names, but a few still clung to her memory. One in particular: General Blake Patton. He was a gentle soul with a loud voice. He took a lot of ribbing from his men because of his name. They would ask him to sing a Blake Shelton country song or sometimes they made swords out of cardboard and would wear them at their side, to mock the famous "Patton Sword." Even though they pretended to poke fun at him, Molly had noticed the respect his unit gave him as they came one by one to visit him. He may have had the rank of a General, but he allowed them to laugh and forget their own troubles, at his expense. He was the kindest and strongest man she had ever met. She hoped he was still alive and could facilitate her proposed project.

Chapter 2

##

Max Callahan leaned back in his chair and stretched his legs. His six-foot body length seemed cramped even under his "custom-made, just for him" desk. Every hour he did his little stretches, just to keep from getting leg cramps. He had been bothered by the nasty spasms while in the Army, and the medic had given him an easy exercise, that if done, often seemed to deter the painful tightening of his leg muscles. Sitting at his desk for extended periods of time, without moving, was like inviting the pain to appear. Doctors had insisted that he see a physical therapist, but he had come to terms with the pain, and had developed his own form of therapy.

A challenge more difficult than the physical pain he experienced was the emotional anguish he suffered every time a cramp occurred. His mind would automatically return to Afghanistan. The shooting pain in his legs was the reason he had fallen during an attack in the village. Crouched by an open doorway, behind a pile of rubbish, a suicide bomber for the enemy carried a grenade launcher in his arms. Max had struggled to run but a fierce spasm had smacked his leg and he went down. He remembered little after that except the smell of peroxide.

He looked at the stack of paperwork he had finished, just since the office had closed and everyone had gone home for the day. He could not believe how much work he could get done after hours, in the quiet. He had come to the office late today, so he felt it was only right that he stayed past working hours. But now the noiseless office seemed strange and unbelievably loud. He was hearing things he guessed he usually took for granted. Like his heart battering against his ears and the tick, tick of the clock. He flinched as the single radiator clanked, hissed and spit steam into the air. How long had that been going on? Why had he never taken notice to these common everyday noises before? He was a man who thrived on details and yet he had missed all these sounds.

He took a short stroll around his desk, just to loosen his leg muscles, and stopped in front of the window. A sudden peal of thunder and a silvery flash of lightning filled the room bringing with it rain that lashed against the windowpanes. Strong winds were driving the rain horizontally as lightning continued to slither across the dark sky. People on the sidewalk below were trying to run. He felt helpless as he watched a woman and her coat begin a tug-of-war with the intense wind gusts. Another loud crack of thunder boomed overhead causing the woman to take a nervous step backward and fall from the curb.

Max ran down the three flights of steps and unlocked the front door. He called out to the woman, but the howl of the wind prevented her from hearing him. She tried to stand, but a gust of wind knocked her down again.

Needle-sharp rain peppered Max as he reached down and gathered the soaking-wet woman in his arms and carried her inside the building. Caught off-guard by his actions, she squirmed under his piercing-dark gaze and shoved an elbow in his ribs. She struggled to keep her voice calm and steady as she spoke. "Thank you for rescuing me, but please put me down!" Brittle, jagged pieces of memory from another dark night slid through her brain. She would not allow herself to be in that position again.

He dropped his hands and stepped back. She quickly backed up also, trying to get a good look at him, and realized he was dressed in a suit. He grabbed three towels from the nearby bathroom and gave her two, keeping one for himself.

He held out his hand as he said, "Hi, I'm Max Callahan. I work on the third floor of this building and obviously was working late tonight, when I saw the wind take hold of you. I ran down to try and help you. No need to be afraid."

"Yea, that's what the last guy said." As soon as the words popped out of her mouth, Molly regretted saying them. No one, not even her family knew of her "ordeal." She had convinced herself that it was forgotten and tucked away in a far place. But this dark, rainy night had brought the nightmare back to the surface.

"I'm sorry, miss, for whatever happened, but I assure you I'm no threat. I can call you a cab…"

Molly interrupted. "I don't need a cab. I have my car, right around the corner and I'm going there right now."

Sounding frustrated, Max added, "Suit yourself, but my offer stands."

The rich timbre of his voice was like an echo from an empty tomb. Why was it so familiar? The hallway they were standing in was dimly lit, keeping her from getting a good look at this man, but something about him was stirring memories. She took a deep breath against the panic, dropped the wet towels on a nearby table and walked hurriedly to the door. She opened it and ran as fast as she could. The rain was still beating the pavement, but the wind wasn't as fierce, as she found her way to the car. She slid in behind the steering wheel and locked the doors. Within minutes she was on the highway, heading towards home.

With the garage door remote, Molly put the door up and down as fast as she could. She was normally not the spooky kind, but tonight her intuitions had felt threatened. Had this guy, by the name of Max, been watching her from his window or was it just coincidental, like he said? He seemed nice enough. Maybe it was just the thunder and lightning that set the tone for her eerie feeling. Whatever it was, she knew she would feel better after a good night's sleep.

Chapter 3

Max's mother had died of cancer, just three years ago and he had never known his father. When he was younger, he would try to start conversations about his family history, but his mother would always say, "Max, someday when you're older, we'll sit down and I'll tell you about my childhood, but for now, just be happy. There's nothing any of us can do about history. It's a thing of the past."

But the past haunted Max. His mothers' comments made him think she was hiding something. When she got sick, he just didn't have the heart to pressure her into storytelling. She suffered from bad reactions to the chemo and her memory had become jumbled. By that time, he realized it was too late for him to inquire about days gone by. If he wanted to know, he would have to find another way.

Max lived alone in a small, but modern apartment and often talked out loud to himself. He liked to pretend that Charlie could understand what he was saying. So, tonight was no different when he walked in to find the mutt eagerly awaiting his return. The tail wagging, the kisses; it was all a ritual the two friends performed. It was very comforting to Max to know that he had been missed, even if it was only by a dog.

As an only child, he had learned to carry on conversations with his stuffed animals. Although none ever answered him, he felt a sense of communication with the fluffy audience. Talking out-loud, to himself, had become a habit, even in his adult years. He gave Charlie a full run-down of the evening's events, waiting for some reaction, but the dog turned his head away from Max and closed his eyes. Max ruffled the top of Charlie's head and sighed with exasperation, "I didn't even find out her name. How pathetic is that?"

Max found a piece of left-over pizza in the fridge and sat down in front of the TV. He popped the cap on the cold beer and took a big swig. What was wrong with him anyhow? He worked every day, even on weekends. He tried to tell himself that he didn't want a relationship but deep down he knew that wasn't true. The few women he had dated seemed to have control issues or they were too wild for his lifestyle. Why couldn't he find someone who still believed that man was head of the household? Not that he wanted total control, he just wanted respect. Something he had never seen his mother give to a man, causing him to make that a number one attraction for a relationship. He knew so many marriages fell apart because there was no appreciation of each other. He had decided a long time ago that he would rather be single and lonely as opposed to married and disrespected. It's not what Webster would say, but respect, in his mind, was a synonym for trust. And he would settle for no less.

Chapter 4

MOLLY

Molly reached over and hit the snooze button. It couldn't be six o'clock already. It seemed like she had just gone to bed. She needed ten more minutes and she would be ready to start her day. But an image of the man from last night seemed to overtake her thoughts, and she sat straight up in bed. Who was he and why was he invading her sleep this morning? Reluctantly, she touched the cold floor with her feet and shivered.

As she walked to the kitchen for her morning cup of tea, she noticed her soaking wet coat laying across the couch; another reminder of last night. She put the coat on a hanger and hung it in the bathroom to dry. She finished her tea while getting dressed, put the empty cup in the sink and opened the garage door. She had never been late for work and this morning would be no different.

When offered the position of Director of Nurses, at the local hospital, she had informed the Board she would accept on one condition. Even though she knew it was mandatory for all personnel to park in the hospital parking garage, she could not agree to that one stipulation due to her fear of dark, secluded spaces. To most, not parking in the hospital garage was a petty request, but to someone who's life had changed because of a humiliating and horrifying experience, it was reason enough to never test fate again.

The board had agreed to her one condition and had provided a designated parking spot on the west side which meant walking by the same building she had passed twice a day for the past two years. The building with the mysterious man who had rescued her from the storm. Today, she didn't want to come anywhere near it, but she had no choice. Realizing it wasn't the brick and mortar she was worried about, but the man from the third floor, she wore her hoodie and jogged past the front door. There would be no way he would recognize her.

For the next two weeks Molly followed the same routine to and from work. From the time she stepped off the elevator until late afternoon when she walked out the front door of the hospital, nothing was more important than her patients and her staff. There was no time for thinking about the man who had rescued her. Each day she thought of him less and less until the only time he came to mind was when she walked past his building. She sometimes wondered if he was standing at his window watching for her. But why would he? She had been rude to him and had made it clear to him she didn't need rescuing. Each time she walked beneath his window, she wanted to look up, but self-respect over-powered the temptation.

"Miss Carlson, Dr. Peterson needs you in his office right away".

"Please, Hannah, please call me Molly. It might be against protocol here, but if my nurses are going to work together and be a team, me included, then we need to be on a first name basis. It helps establish a family atmosphere around here."

"Okay, Molly. I'll spread the word."

"Thanks. Could you see that Joe Miller, in room 105 gets his medicine? I was just about to do that."

"Sure thing."

Molly knocked on Dr. Peterson's door and walked in. She shaded her eyes from the bright sunlight coming through the open curtains. She squinted as she tried to recognize the man sitting in front of the doctor's desk. When he turned to introduce himself, surprise rendered him speechless. It was her, the girl from the rainstorm.

With all the bright light, Molly could see his face. And quite an attractive face it was! The shadow of his beard gave him a most masculine appearance, matching the color of his dark curly hair. It was cut short, tapered neatly to his collar. His eyes, the color of gun metal, widened in shock.

"It's you! I had no idea you worked here."

"Really? Then why are you here?"

"I didn't come to find you if that's what you think. I'm here on business. My company supplies this hospital with a lot of medical equipment."

Dr. Peterson observed the questioning gaze that passed between them and interrupted with a question of his own. "You two know each other?"

Both came back with different answers. Max said yes, while Molly replied with a strong no.

Dr. Peterson leaned forward in his chair and added, "I'm not exactly sure what is going on here but the two of you need to take it out of my office." He stood, straightened his shoulders and sighed loudly, "I asked you to come in here, Molly, because as Director of Nurses, you have knowledge of everything that goes on here with the nursing staff. Mr. Callahan has brought us some very innovative products, hoping to make your job a little less stressful. I would like you to look them over and indicate which ones you feel might be a fit for this hospital. The Board meets next week, and I would like to have the list ready so that I might submit the requisition to them at that time." He continued in a preoccupied tone, "I am needed in surgery so you may use my office to hear Mr. Callahan's presentation. Please be sure to shut the door when you are finished." He picked up his cup of coffee and left the office.

Max was the first to speak. "Are you really so afraid of me? No one has ever told me I resemble Charles Manson."

Molly looked at him with something very fragile in her eyes. He noticed it immediately and apologized.

"I didn't mean to sound so condescending. I've just never had a woman react to me the way you have." His apologetic tone surprised her, and she tossed him a guarded look. "It's really none of your business why I reacted the way I did."

"You're right, and once again I apologize. Could I make it up to you over a cup of coffee?"

A haunting and horrible sense of insecurity swept over Molly as she tried to come up with an excuse why she couldn't go out with this good-looking man, but everything she thought of sounded very childish. "Let's take care of business before we talk about anything else. Dr. Peterson will have my head if I don't take the time to see what you have to offer."

The next hour was spent talking about new ways to save patient's data. Readings were not currently being sent to the patient's physician, causing delays in urgent diagnosis. Max's company had found a way to communicate the data back to the patient's physician within hours. It was impressive. He showed Molly the latest in stethoscopes and allowed her to listen to the high acoustic sensitivity as he placed it on his own chest.

As she listened to his heart, she flashed him a sweet smile and said, "Maybe I should have you admitted. Your heart seems to be beating rather fast. Have you been experiencing shortness of breath lately?"

Max grinned sheepishly and cleared his throat. "Can't say that I have. Maybe it's because of my present surroundings."

He waited for Molly to answer but instead she removed the stethoscope from around her neck, placed it back in the box and as her tone hardened, she replied tartly, "If we decide to submit an order, you'll be hearing from us." She turned and walked out the door.

What was it about this woman with red hair that interested him so? She was the most egotistical female he had ever met. From the first time he noticed her, his only intention had been to help her. Even today, yes, he had tried to sell his wares, but he also had genuinely tried to help her and her staff become more proficient at their job. He was proud of his company and the integrity they tried to maintain. It wasn't an easy business, given the constant reminder of hospital budgets. They all wanted the product, but budget cuts were a major issue. Sometimes a tragedy had to occur before they would allow a new product to be introduced into their program.

Max knew his company was on the cutting edge of technology, was good at negotiating and usually worked well with the doctors and personnel. He also knew he was good at his job and had never been dismissed as he had been today. He packed up his samples and found his way out of the hospital. Keeping his company's account alive at Willow Grove would test his endurance as a salesman. If Molly Carlson continued as head nurse, he would simply hand over the account to his partner, Wayne.

Molly left Dr. Peterson's office and slipped quietly into the nurse's bathroom. She splashed water on her face, hoping to take away the flush of embarrassment she felt. The man was just doing his job and so what if he flirted? Why did she react so immature? She was a grown woman who had many men flirt with her in the past and today she acted like a real jerk. She knew a compliment when she heard one, and she had heard one today; she just hadn't appreciated the presenter.

Molly's phone was ringing when she opened her front door. It was her therapist asking if she could come in to see her this evening at seven o'clock. Molly thought briefly about cancelling, but decided against it. She needed to continue with her therapy. She was desperate to figure out how not to be so vulnerable with her personal life.

"Good evening, Molly. Thank you for accommodating my timeline and coming a day early. How are you tonight?"

Molly hated these sessions and she loved them. Since Afghanistan, she had been reluctant to get close to anyone.

One reason the Army had set up these treatments was to help reduce her paranoia and find relief from her Post Trauma Stress Disorder she had been suffering with since returning from overseas.

Nursing had been a dream of Molly's ever since she could remember. As a young girl she had set up a makeshift hospital in her bedroom and administered many shots to her dolls. She smiled as she thought about it now, thankful they couldn't feel her stabs to their behinds. Money was tight in her parent's household and the chance of her attending college was out of the question. Her father had "old school" ideas about women going to college. He was a firm believer that women didn't need a college degree. His favorite saying was "Women don 't need books to teach them how to clean the house and take care of their man." Molly cringed as she thought of all the times she had heard her father bellow that to her mother.

Army recruiters had visited Molly's high school and she had found herself intrigued with their presentation. The prestige of being a commissioned officer and having someone respect her was very enticing. She collected all the pamphlets and information that day, took them home, read and reread each one until she had convinced herself this was what she wanted to do. She knew her dad would not handle the news well but in time she hoped he would respect her decision.

After school the next day she went straight to the recruiter's office downtown and signed up. She had just celebrated her eighteenth birthday, so a parent's signature wasn't required. She would leave for basic training in Texas, one week after graduation. She couldn't wait to give her family the news and hope they would be proud of her. If they weren't, she had a great feeling about her decision and for the first time in her life, she was looking forward to her future.

Chapter 5

MOLLY

Molly had been early for her therapy session, praying no one would see how badly her hands were shaking. She chose a chair in the far corner of the waiting room, anticipating the next hour with Nancy Carter, the therapist. She was a woman with curves that didn't need the help of fancy clothes; they made themselves known, no matter what she wore. Sometimes Molly just stared at the woman's bosom, wondering how she carried so much weight and remained upright.

The receptionist called Molly's name twice before she heard her. She stood and walked into Ms. Carter's office. Scolding herself silently for concerning herself about her therapist's breasts, she neglected to acknowledge Ms. Carter's first remarks.

"I feel as if you're a bit distant this evening, Molly. Is there something specifically bothering you?"

"I'm sorry, Ms. Carter, what did you say?"

"Please call me Nancy, and it's obvious something specific is troubling you tonight. Would you like to talk about it?"

Molly wanted to smile because of what she had been thinking about, but Nancy's physical appearance was not what she had come here tonight to discuss. Smiling might confuse Nancy's evaluation of her.

A sigh leaked out of Molly like air from a punctured tire, but she spoke no words, nor did she smile. Her focus had shifted to a dark place, her downcast expression pleading for understanding. Nancy silently questioned the unusual change in her behavior but remained quiet. She wanted Molly to talk when she was ready.

There had been some major break-throughs last week with Molly's anxiety and Nancy was hoping for the same discussion to continue. The obvious internal battle this young woman was struggling with, needed to be resolved. Molly was a woman proud of her independence and especially of her past position as a nurse in the United States Army, but whatever had happened in Afghanistan was rooted deep in her existence.

As Molly's therapist for the past year, Nancy was sure about that deep dark secret, and she wanted so desperately to help her, but Molly was strong-willed and did things on her own time schedule. Nancy had noticed simple things, like a slight squint of the eye, a sideways movement of her jaw when specific subjects were brought into the conversation. These physical, nervous ticks were always visible when she allowed her sub-conscious to surface.

Molly always spoke with pride when reliving a successful operation or when a soldier's limb had been saved, but the amputations, the image of a young man's guts trailing behind him instead of inside him, brought tears and the visible physical movements. Nancy had recognized something even more profound; an unshakable, undesirable burden hidden deep within Molly's character. So deep, she was emotionally unaware of the havoc it was declaring on her body. Her physical appearance tonight seemed more exhausted and broken than usual.

Nancy knew an important step in Molly's relief of her past battle scars was she must first recognize the hurt. This girl had obviously suffered significant emotional trauma and time was of the essence if she were going to help Molly find peace with her combat memories. Provoking those emotional involvements of wounded comrades and body bags stuffed with remains was not a pleasant remembrance, but a necessary evil towards recovery. Nancy had listened to Molly talk about those she had befriended while enjoying a meal together, or listening to stories of their hometown, only to find them come back to camp in body bags.

Molly had seen so much, witnessed too many painful scenes and she needed time to erase the pain. It had been two years since she had returned to the United States and even though it was in her past, those memories were still raw. Nancy's advice, "time only goes in one direction" was ingrained in Molly's mind as she constantly thought of the enemy, hidden grenades and snipers. But another inner torment kept gnawing at her, eating at her from the inside. Time may only go in one direction but sometimes it stood still for Molly, trapping her inside the compound with sounds of gunfire and explosions. She was also trapped with sounds of her own screams and memories of a dark building where she was attacked and lost her innocence. She could still smell the whiskey on his breath and feel the belt buckle, cold against her skin. Sometimes she felt as if that one night was more traumatic than the other three-hundred and twenty-five days she spent living in a war. Maybe it was time to tell Nancy the real reason she was here.

In her previous therapy sessions Molly thought she had fooled Nancy with her chirpy little tone, but she knew she needed to be done with pretending. She was craving to spill her guts and see what happened. Knowing what she knew and the fact that the secret she had been keeping might cost her the freedom she so loved, she still felt the need to speak out.

Chapter 6

Max finished the proposal for the hospital contract, sat back and massaged the back of his neck. He experienced physical pain every time he entered another number into the computer. Would the bid to the hospital be low enough to meet with the board's budget or was all this work for nothing? How much influence did Ms. Carlson have with the board members and would she try to sabotage his execution of this deal? He had put extra hours into this project, hoping to win the bid, but also to impress Ms. Carlson. He was suddenly feeling uncomfortable with the fact that he cared what this woman thought. Even though he acknowledged the maddening hint of arrogance about her, he smiled with warm spontaneity. Whether he wanted to admit it or not, he was wildly attracted to Miss Molly Carlson.

Max shut down the computer and drove home. His answering machine was blinking, and Charlie was waiting, ready to run through their routine. He left the dog out the back door and returned to the living room to listen to his messages. The first and second ones were telemarketers, but the third one caught his attention. "Hi. I'm looking for a Maxwell Callahan. My name is Bruce Watkins. I live in Kentucky and I think we are related. Would you call me back if your mother's name was Isabella Priscilla Callahan? My number is 602-555-1312. I'm working on a family tree for school and I'd really appreciate your help. Thanks, Max."

What a strange request. Max had never heard of this kid, but then he knew none his family. "I'm going to take you back to your roots someday" is all he ever heard from his mother. She had stories to tell him about his maternal grandparents and a few aunts, but he wasn't sure she hadn't made them up. He had never been to a family reunion or ever enjoyed Christmas or Easter dinner with anyone other than his mother. He always thought she was doing the best she could, but the older he got, the more he recognized her talent for keeping secrets.

Eager for some family history, Max picked up the phone and dialed the Kentucky number. His mother's full name was Isabella Priscilla Callahan, and how many women could there be with that name?

"Hello."

"My name is Max Callahan and I'm calling for a Bruce Watkins."

"Hi Max, this is Bruce. I hope you're calling to tell me that we're related. I've just about given up on this family tree project."

Max stifled the urge to laugh, "Unless you've found someone else who had a mother with the name of Isabella Priscilla, I think you've found your man."

A thin thread of hysteria in Bruce's voice told Max this young man was genuinely excited and his easy laugh spoke well of him.

"I can't believe I'm really talking to Max, son of Isabella. My mother, Alice, and your mother were sisters, which makes us first cousins."

The shock of the announcement hit Max full force. All these years with no extended family and just like that, he's told he has a cousin. "You're my cousin? How old are you?"

"I just turned twenty. How old are you?"

"I'm twenty-seven and I can't believe I have a cousin." Max swallowed hard, trying not to reveal his resentment. "Why have I never heard of you before?"

Searching for a plausible explanation, Bruce chose his words carefully "I had no idea that you were not aware of my existence. Does that mean that you don't know any of your relatives?"

Max tried to force his confused emotions in order, "You mean I have other relatives?"

Bruce's head swirled with questions? "You mean you never heard of any of us?" I know your mother took you away when you were just a baby, but I guess we all assumed she would have at least told you about your family. We always wondered why you never came to visit us."

Max met Bruce's question with one of his own, "Why did you never come to visit me, or at least call?"

The words he heard next chilled Max to the bone. "Because your mother made it very clear to everyone in the family that if we ever tried to contact you, she would kill herself." He hesitated, torn by conflicting emotions.

"I'm sorry, Max, the family was convinced she would carry out her threat and no one wanted to bear the responsibility of calling her bluff. Somehow my mother found out that she had passed away and felt it would be alright now for me to follow through on this project. I'm sorry about your mother and the fact that we've never met. I'm really looking forward to getting to know you."

Max gritted his teeth and fought down the snarl of anger nearly choking him. How could his mother impose such an injustice against him? She had been a great force in his life, giving him everything he had ever needed, to include her support in all his activities. But obviously she had a selfish side to her. Why had she never allowed him to love or be loved by other family members. He found it all disturbing.

"I'm gonna have to call you back, Bruce. I can't quite wrap my head around this information."

Not expecting such a sudden end to their conversation, Bruce was startled when he heard the click of the receiver. Max sounded like a nice enough guy, but maybe discovering relatives was more than he could handle. Bruce had no idea what was going on in his cousin's life right now. He didn't even ask if he was married. But that was just one of the many questions on his list.

Bruce waited a few days for Max to call back. Rejection was not something he handled well and especially by a family member, a recognized one or not. If he had to, he would drive to Tennessee and find Max in person. Not only for his school project, but for the family. Everyone had seemed excited when they discovered they had another cousin. Always room at the reunions for one more they said. Isabella and Max had always been a topic of discussion at family gatherings but the two had always remained a mystery. Everyone had a theory as to why Isabella had left Kentucky and why she had never returned. Until now, Max had just been a fantasy. Wouldn't it be great to finally meet this long-lost cousin!

Even though Max had to push only a button to hang up, he slammed the phone to the floor, more in frustration than anger. Why would his mother have kept all this family stuff a secret? Was he illegitimate or was she ashamed of him? What could have been so dreadful that she hid him from family. When he was younger, he used to question her about his father, but she would cry and he would console her and get no information. He finally quit asking, hoping she would someday be ready to tell him, but time passed, and the story went untold. Now he had a chance to find the truth and he was hesitating. He weighed the pros and cons of his dilemma. What if he met his family and they all hated him or rejected him? What if Bruce was the only one who would talk to him, and that was because of his school project.

He wasn't sure he could handle any more stress in his life at this time. Maybe he should just pretend he had never heard of Bruce Watkins. The fewer people in his life meant fewer problems to deal with. He had survived for twenty-seven years without extended family so he could surely continue the same way. He was curious, but life wasn't so bad right now. He had a good job and was even trying to figure out how to ask Molly Carlson on a date. She had generated a cocktail of emotions within him, leaving him in an unnerving situation. And now this.

A primitive instinct of self-preservation kicked in and Max picked up the phone again, dialed Bruce's number and left a message. "Bruce, I'd like to talk to you some more about my mother. Please call me back. Thanks." He warmed up last night's leftovers, changed into sweatpants and waited for the phone call that would change his life forever.

Chapter 7

MOLLY

Silence hung heavy in the air as Nancy waited for some response from her patient. She got the feeling that Molly was nearly at a breakthrough, but she didn't want to rush it. She watched as Molly's stare focused on the shadows on the wall caused by the flickering flames from the fireplace.

"Molly, would you like to talk about something different tonight? Did something else happen to you while in Afghanistan besides your nursing encounters?"

Leaning forward, Molly clasped her hands together and rocked. Soon she was shaking and sobbing uncontrollably. Her face betrayed a definite struggle, such as a secret held rigidly under control and was now about to explode. Her voice was cold as she spit out the words disrespectfully. "I told him NO and I screamed, but no one heard me, especially him."

"Someo "Is there more that I need to understand Molly?"

Nancy saw something flickering far back in Molly's watery eyes, like dark smoldering ashes. She was silenced by her patient's dark, angry expression as she watched this young woman's pride try to conceal the turbulence within her.

Molly feared the emotional black wall she had created around her for protection was crumbling. She knew she had allowed fear to make strangers of people she wanted to be friends with. Like Max Callahan. He appeared to be a nice guy, but as he rushed out of that dark building into the storm that dark night, pretending to be Superman, an uncomfortable haunting impulse had caused a tight place of anxiety in her heart. Max's action was a carbon copy of the night in Afghanistan. The darkness and blustery weather brought on by a storm, the place of shelter offered by a man – it was all the same scenario. The only difference was that Max had not been in uniform. However, the encounter still brought back the memory of the soldier who lurked in the shadows of her mind.

Molly answered Nancy's question with a shake of her head, screwed up her face and yelled, "YES, he raped me". She leaned forward, lowered her voice and with a threatening quality, she spoke, "He was an officer, someone with authority, someone we all trusted. He used his influence to stifle my testimony and my future as a nurse. Said it was his word against mine and who would believe a nurse over a Lieutenant?"

Nancy thought Molly's PTSD was from too much war but now she knew her pain was much more personal. She may have escaped with her virtue, but her innocence had been left behind. Just because a man wore a uniform and exuded some power, did not give him a license to cause such devastation in a young woman's life. No wonder she wasn't interested in a relationship.

"Molly, I know you want to forget what happened, but until you acknowledge it, it will just keep screaming louder until it has your full attention. Have you ever said out loud that you were raped, before tonight? " Folding her hands in a pose of tranquility, Nancy continued, " I know it sounds scary at first, but trust me, it will eventually give you power."

Raising her chin, Molly assumed all the dignity she could find. "Power? Power for what?"

Nancy continued with gentle sureness, knowing she needed to choose her next words carefully. "The power I'm talking about Molly is the power you have for yourself. Nurturing yourself is very important, and by that, I mean be kind to yourself. You shouldn't say anything to yourself that you wouldn't say to a friend who was raped. Be gentle and patient to yourself. You have the power to do those things, Molly. Go to exercise class, buy yourself some flowers, take a two-hour bubble-bath. Those are things you have control over and things that will help you overcome some fear. You may think this all sounds crazy, but given some time, it will help. Nothing ever takes away the memory of what happened to you and the old saying about time heals is not just a cliché- it's true. Time heals what reason cannot. It's already been a few years since this happened to you and I'm sure you're more than ready for healing. And because you are now ready to talk about it, the healing process can finally begin."

Molly's feelings took over for a moment and tears of fright gathered in the corner of her eyes. She once again felt threatened by the strangeness she was feeling. She didn't want to be a martyr. She wanted to be a survivor.

Molly | 33

Sitting here, she knew she was floundering, reluctant to expose her emotions. Baring her soul was so out of character for her. She was used to thinking that women who cried were very needy people and tears were a waste of time; they threatened to rob a person of their control. Now here she sat with tears trickling down her cheeks like rain running down the window. As the pain resurfaced, a tortured sob escaped, giving way to the great heaving sobs that wracked her body. She would need time to deal with these contradictory emotions.

Nancy handed her a box of tissues while she spoke softly, trying to dispense hope and healing with her words. Even though Molly's confidence felt as fragile as eggshells, she mentally gathered her courage, finding a rebellious pleasure in the challenge of becoming a committed survivor. Her cheeks burned in remembrance, crimson with resentment and humiliation, but with the sense of conviction that was part of her character. She knew she was now on the road to recovery.

Since the night of terror, two years ago, the flood gates were finally open, allowing the torment to find its way out of her domain. Just knowing that someone else now knew her suffering gave Molly a sense she could begin her return to life as she used to know it. It was time to stop looking back and holding on to the pain.

Nancy brought a cup of hot tea and sat it on the table beside Molly, hoping she would take a few sips. Specifics of the night in Afghanistan had not yet been revealed, but in time, Nancy knew Molly would unwrap the details and eventually accept more help.

A tidal wave of hope had swept over Molly and she wanted Nancy to know how deeply indebted she felt for her kindness. The night in Afghanistan had damaged her confidence and scarred her heart, but now that she knew there was help for her, she felt a small but satisfying victory.

Chapter 8

MAX

Waiting for the phone call from his "cousin" was very nerve-wracking for Max. The young man had seemed so excited and eager to talk, yet here it was, two days later and he had not responded to Max's message.

Max laughed out loud as he watched Charlie try to manipulate his blanket into just the right folds. He was always so particular about this process. "Could you please lie down Charlie? I have some things I need to talk to you about." The dog laid down and waited for Max to talk. "Why do you think this guy who says he's my cousin, hasn't called back? Do you think he didn't like my voice?" Charlie barked, rolled over and shut his eyes. Max took that as a sign that the conversation was over.

Within minutes the phone rang, and Max ran to pick it up. "Hi. Is this Max?"

"Yea, this is Max. Bruce? I was beginning to think you hadn't got my message."

"Sorry about that cuz but I'm swamped with midterms. I had to get them finished before I could continue with this family tree project. I was glad to hear from you though. Are you ready to answer some questions? Your family wants to know all about you and what you've been doing all these years."

"I'm the one who wants to ask questions. I can't believe I really have a family."

"Well you do and you're welcome anytime. Here's my address if you want to come visit."

Max took the information and promised to keep in touch. The minute he hung up he knew what he would do. He pulled out a map, targeted the little town of Corbin and figured out how long it would take him to get there.

He searched all weekend for information about this small town in Kentucky. It sounded like a great place to live. Why would his mother take him away from his home and family, bring him to a big city and raise him all alone? Had something happened that would cause such a rift in the family? He didn't know the answers, but he needed to find out. Suddenly, out of the blue something came to mind. A flowered box his mother kept on the top shelf of her closet. He had been tempted often to open it, but she had made him promise he would never look inside. He had every right to look now, but where was it? He took a minute to reflect on the days after his mother's death and tried to jog his memory. It was a bright colored box. He needed to remember it. There were a few boxes in his basement that the auction house had deemed personal. Maybe they had saved it.

He slit the tape on each box until he found what he was looking for. He couldn't open it fast enough. Inside were pictures. Pictures of aunts and uncles, cousins and even grandparents. Names had been written on the back along with dates and places. Some as recent as five years ago. He looked quickly to see if Bruce might be among the relatives but no one by that name was listed. Digging deeper in the box he found letters from his mother's sister Alice, Bruce's mother. There were also a few letters from his grandparents. The ink had faded, and the paper was crumbly, but Max laid them out on the table and read each one. There was nothing very personal, nothing to indicate the writer was a relative of the recipient. There were also two letters addressed to Isabella Callahan. The name on the return address was Silas Cooper.

Max lowered himself into the nearest chair, with these two letters in hand. He tried to carry on another conversation with Charlie, but the dog didn't seem interested. He spoke out loud anyhow, ignoring the dogs' mood. "Could this have been from my father? The writing is rather intimate, for the time period. But whoever Silas was, he was in love with my mother. Why did she choose a life of loneliness over the likelihood of being married and having a family?"

He continued looking through the box, finding only a few pieces of old jewelry and about a dozen lace handkerchiefs. As he lifted them up, a picture of a young man in a white Naval dress uniform with his arm around Max's mother fell out from between the layers.

Still pretending Charlie was listening, Max persisted on relating the rest of the story to him. "Look at this, Charlie, maybe this guy is my father. What do you think?" Charlie opened one eye, yawned and went back to sleep. The writing on the back of the picture said "Love, Silas.

Love, Silas. If this was his father, he was a man of few words. No extra sentiments like I miss you, or I'll love you forever – just Love, Silas.

Max gave out a short laugh, filled with embarrassment, when he realized how much he relied on a reaction from a dog. But then, everyone knew Charlie wasn't your average dog. Max honestly believed he had a brain comparable to some humans.

He took the picture and clipped it to the front of the fridge, as a souvenir of days gone by. Days when his mother must have been happy and looking forward to a bright future. What had happened to her dreams and Silas? Why had they both disappeared?

Max returned the remaining contents to the box and carried it to the dining room table. It would be part of his luggage when he left for Corbin. Somebody, somewhere, had to give him answers.

He called his partner, Wayne, and ask if he could manage for a while without him. He filled him in with the information about the hospital account and warned him of Miss Carlson's attitude, assuring him it was a personal matter, nothing against the company. He reminded Wayne of the importance of the account.

With Wayne's blessing he packed his suitcase, got out the map from the glove compartment and sat down to find the shortest and fastest way to Corbin.

"Are you ready for a road trip Charlie?" Max laughed as the dog ran in circles, a good indication he was eager to go. With everything needed for the trip loaded into the trunk, Max opened the door, allowing Charlie to jump on the front seat and snuggle down into his blanket.

Driving to Corbin allowed Max time to reflect on what he was doing. Driving to a place he had never been before to see people he didn't know. That sounded a little crazy, but Bruce had enticed him with his more than friendly approach. Max was curious. He had always thought it would be great to have a large family, but his mother had squashed that reality with her secretiveness. The odds of discovering he had relatives, especially after his mother's death, was high on the list of not happening, so when Bruce called and Max discovered there was only two hours distance between them, it was quite a shock. He couldn't quit asking the question of why didn't he know? Why had his mother hidden such important information from him?

As he pulled into the roadside rest area to let Charlie lift his leg on a tree, he noticed a Corbin, Kentucky bumper sticker stuck in the back window of a pickup. He allowed the dog to take care of business and then waited for the owner. As soon as Max saw the old man exit the restrooms, he knew he was looking at the owner of the truck.

"Excuse me sir, but according to your sticker, you are from Corbin?"

With a deep tobacco-ridden voice he answered. "Yea. Do I know you?"

"No. Well, maybe." Max pointed to the dog and said, "Charlie and I are headed there right now. I recently found out I have relatives living there and I'm going to meet them."

"So, what's the name of your kin?"

"I'm not exactly sure of all of them but my mother's maiden name was Callahan."

The man's mouth dropped open and Max sensed a quick tensing of the man's body. He looked like he was about to faint.

"Are you alright sir?" I have some water in my car."

"No thank ya, I'm fine. Just leaned on my bad leg a little too hard. So, you say you're goin to Corbin. Nice little town. Lived there all my life. Know everbody within twenty miles. Max felt everything go silent inside him except for his heart thumping against his rib cage. "Could I ask you a question Mr. – I'm sorry I don't know your name."

"Everone just calls me Diggor".

Max held out an open hand, "Nice to meet you Diggor. My name is Max and my four-legged friend here is Charlie. Maybe we'll see you around town someday."

"Yea, maybe." Digger couldn't seem to get in his car fast enough. He started the engine and drove out of the parking lot as if someone were chasing him. Was it Max's imagination or was that old man in a hurry to get away from him?

Chapter 9

SHERIFF BAXTER

"Hey Diggor, where ya been all day?"

The old man's big, droopy eyes stared at Sheriff Baxter with notable coldness. There was no need for him to speak; his face spoke for him.

Peering over his black rimmed glasses, the Sheriff lifted one dark brow and with annoyance present in his voice said, "I asked you a question, Diggor, where ya been? Did you find your wife with an old boyfriend or what?" Noting the anxious look on the old man's face, Sheriff Baxter stood from his chair and walked towards Diggor. Even though he spoke in a softer tone, there was credible strength in his words, "I'm gonna ask you one more time. What happened out there today?"

Icy fear twisted around Diggor's heart. What he saw today was enough to cause him another heart-attack. He swallowed hard, trying to manage an answer, if only a weak one. His boss was waiting. He had to say something.

"I went for a drive today and stopped at the rest stop in Laurel County to take a pee and when I came out of the bathroom this guy was waiting for me by my truck. It was a good thing that I had already drained the lizard, or I would have peed my pants right there."

Baxter was getting irritated with Digger's drawn-out version of a most-likely exaggerated rumor. Lately it seemed like most of Digger' stories were a lot of gossip.

"Okay, Digger, who was it? Santa Claus, or maybe the Easter Bunny?"

Digger glowered indignantly at the Sheriff while he cleared his throat of rumbling phlegm. "It was Max Callahan."

Baxter felt the blood drain from his face, "Max Callahan? Are you sure?"

"Sure as I'm standin here. Shook my hand even!"

"Is he headed here to Corbin?"

"Yep. Said he was comin to meet some of his kin."

"Who would have told him and how did they find him?"

"I don't know, Boss, but what are you gonna do?"

"I'm gonna do nothing till I find out what he knows, or what anybody knows, for that matter. We don't want to act like we know something. When he shows up, we're going to act like we don't know a thing."

When Diggor didn't answer, Baxter considered his toothless smile a badge of honor.

Baxter looked up to Deputy John Diggorty, or 'Diggor' as everyone called him. He had been employed with the County for forty years and was a loyal employee. He was a warrior who had battled hard with cancer and survived three times. He had seen a lot of happenings in Corbin, good and bad, to include the day Max Callahan was born.

Baxter paced the room with long, indecisive strides. He had convinced himself a long time ago this day would never happen. Now that it was here, he was unprepared. Isabella Callahan, at one time, had been the talk of the town. That was twenty-some years ago and even though the Callahan name was still a familiar one in Corbin, he wondered how long it would take people to connect Max's name with Isabella's. Once they did, he was sure the old rumors would be brought back to life and the scuttlebutt would begin.

He had heard that Isabella passed away a few years ago. As far as he knew, there were now only two people in this world who knew the truth. Diggor and himself. Unless! Unless Isabella had shared the story with her son. But if she had, why had Max waited so long after her death to connect to his family. Baxter would have confidence in his instincts that the prodigal son was here by invitation, not because of acquired knowledge.

The town's main intersection, with the only stoplight, was directly in front of the sheriff's office. If he wanted, he could keep track of every car that came through Corbin. He forgot to ask Diggor what kind of vehicle Max was driving, but so far, he had seen no unfamiliar cars drive by this window. Corbin was off the beaten path, so unless you were a resident, there was no reason to drive through the town.

According to Max's GPS, he and Charlie were only a few miles from Corbin. He put his window down and breathed in what he thought would be fresh air, but instead, it was odors of earth and cattle. The manure smell was almost overwhelming, so he pushed the button to close the window. Just in time, as the dust trails following a tractor digging into the soil, drifted across his windshield. Round hay bales sat in the field stubble that became mesmerizing to Max as he drove through this beautiful countryside. He was so absorbed in the surroundings; he never saw the deer until he heard it hit his car door on the passenger side. Fear spiced with irritation gripped Max as he slammed on the brake. Charlie flew to the floor and whimpered. Max leaned over and picked up the dog, making sure he was okay. He turned the car off and jumped out, just in time to see the deer leap over the barbed-wire fence. He was relieved to see that the animal wasn't hurt, but he couldn't say the same about his car. A huge dent had disfigured the door and big clumps of thick brown hair, mixed with blood, was stuck between the door handles and the window. Miraculously, the window had not been broken.

Not sure what to do next, Max returned to the car, allowed Charlie to sit on his lap for a few minutes and then got him settled onto his blanket. Minutes later the big wooden sign welcoming visitors to Corbin came into view, stirring Max's fears and uncertainties to incredible heights.

Following directions, he drove until he found 134 Madison Street. A cute little house of red brick. There was a green hose snaked across the front lawn with the sprinkler fanning water, some spilling over into the flowerbeds. A welcome sign hung by the front door, indicating to Max that hospitality and warmth resided behind these walls. He had never called Bruce with an exact time of his arrival so he wasn't sure if anyone would be home. No one came to the door after ringing the bell, so Max backed out of the driveway and headed back towards town. He wanted to get a first-hand look at where he almost grew up.

As he drove through the tree-lined streets and into the business section of town he drove past an open-air farmers market. He pulled the car to the curb, put a quarter in the meter and walked back to find rows of tables and booths filled with local produce. There were bundles of carrots, bags of potatoes and more zucchini than he had ever seen in one place. There were baskets filled with fruits of every kind, sitting alongside jars of honey and beeswax products. Jelly jars of every size and flavor occupied display stands.

Freshly baked pies, cookies and his favorite whoopie-pies sat waiting for the next hungry customer. Remembering he had had nothing to eat for a few hours, he bought a whoopie-pie. He pulled back the plastic wrap and savored the first bite. Within minutes, he bought five more.

"I guess that tastes pretty good huh? You should probably get a cup of coffee to go with the rest of those!"

Max turned around to see the old man from the rest area. "Diggor, right? How are you? This place is amazing. Is it like this every day?"

"Well I think you are just mighty hungry. All this food starin ya' in the face will make your stomach rumble. Farmer's Market is only Friday and Saturday."

Max smiled to himself as he spoke, "If I lived near here, I would be here every week-end."

"Yea, but after you're here awhile, it gets to be just another day. Not too exciting to us natives. We sorta take it for granted."

"You sure did take off in a hurry at the rest area. I thought I must have said something that insulted you. Did I?"

Stroking his chin, he said, "Nah, I just needed to git home. Not only was my leg actin up but my guts were a tumblin around and I wanted to git home for' I had need of the toilet again." He rubbed his hand across the nape of his neck and resumed his explanation. "When you're old, the only time you can hurry is when nature calls."

Max gave a deep hearty chuckle. This old man reminded him of a good ole boy. It was refreshing to hear someone say what they meant. "Hey Diggor, where's the best place to fill up my car and get a bite to eat? Oh, I need a body shop too. A deer ran into my car, just outside of town."

"Over on the corner of Fourth and Ivy is a great garage. Ask for Hooter and tell him Diggor said he's to take good care of you. Diner's right across the railroad tracks and they've got good food." He pointed down the street and said, "Take a left, can't miss it."

Max spent the rest of the day sightseeing and observing people. Either he was imagining things, or he had a sign stuck to him that said, 'Stare at me'. He looked in the mirror several times to make sure he didn't have something growing out of his nose or a horn protruding from his head. People's stoic expressions gave him no hint as to what they were thinking. Or why?

He drove back to Bruce's house, hoping he had returned and was glad to see a car in the driveway. Before Max could get out of his car, a young man was standing beside him, opening his door.

"Hi Max! I'm so glad to meet you. Come on in and meet my mother and dad. You'll meet everyone else tomorrow at the party. We didn't want to scare you off so we're waiting till tomorrow evening."

Max was so relieved. He felt an instant connection with Bruce. "Is it alright if I bring Charlie in? He's been in the car all day. Could I let him run for a little?"

"Sure, Max." He watched as Max unleased the little Shitzu, allowing him to run from one end of the yard to the other. When he had enough, Charlie came and laid down by Bruce's feet, panting, tongue hanging out, waiting for a drink. "I think he likes me. Come on Charlie, let's get you some water."

Meeting Bruce's parents, Alice and Tom, put Max at ease once again. He was getting anxious to discover why his mother had kept him from these wonderful people.

Chapter 10

MOLLY

Molly's next few therapy visits brought some relief to her PTSD. Just talking about her time in Afghanistan generated reinforcement; that she was not to blame. Nancy wanted her to report the incident, but dredging up those memories in a court room was not something she wanted to do. Besides, so much time had passed, she was sure no one would believe her.

With Nancy's help she worked through her grief and her trust issues with men. She worked a lot of overtime at the hospital, just to keep busy. She believed the more time she spent caring for others, the less time she would have to remember the past. But despite her busy schedule, the memories of the Lieutenant's words, 'If you ever tell anyone, you'll be sorry', returned to haunt her day after day.

Every morning and every evening, as she walked past the three-story brick building, or as she liked to call it "The Haunting", she felt herself being transported right back to Afghanistan. She would tell herself that when she reached the hospital she would go straight to the administrator's office and give her resignation. When ask why, she would simply say she could not deal with the everyday stress of walking by a particular building. By the time she reached the hospital, the reason sounded silly and she didn't want to explain her past. And she didn't want to cause trouble for Max Callahan, the medical supply salesman, so she kept silent. And why was that? What did it matter if he no longer maintained the hospital account? Why should she care what happened to him? That was the problem. She did seem to care. Something about him kept surfacing in her mind. Something so familiar, yet so camouflaged. Questions kept hammering at her. Who was this man and why can't I remember? Speaking out loud, without realizing it, Molly's voice cut the silence. "He must be connected to my Army days, as I always seem to have another round of painful memories come at me when I think of him. I must find another job. Somewhere far from the city and no ghosts from my past"

For the next two weeks Molly searched the internet, looking for a new job in a new town. Hopefully it would be in nursing, but she would take whatever was available. Molly looked on-line one more time before going to bed and then she saw it: Immediate opening for registered nurse in rural area of Kentucky. Must have driver's license and willing to work on weekends. Room and board provided. Only serious calls.

She wrote down the phone number, excited to call first thing tomorrow morning. Night swooped over Molly as she tossed and turned, dreaming of mountains and medicine.

"My name is Molly Carlson and I'm calling about the nursing job. Is it still open?"

"Yes, it is. Would you like to know more about it?"

"Please, I'm very interested. I am currently Director of Nurses at Willow Grove Medical Center in Tennessee. I also served a year in Afghanistan with the Army. Is it possible I could come for an interview?"

The woman on the phone quickly asked, "When can you get here?"

Molly promptly answered, "How about tomorrow at ten?"

Molly requested a personal day and left early for the drive to Corbin, Kentucky. Driving the two hours gave her ample time to practice her interviewing skills. It had been a while since she had been questioned about her nursing abilities.

Driving through the mountains and the lush countryside brought a sense of peace to Molly. The two-lane highway shadowed a small creek with a meandering flow of water. Molly pulled to the side and stepped outside the car, just to hear the trickling water gush around the moss-covered rocks and over fallen twigs. She saw a small fish jump out of the water and grab a flying bug. It was all very soothing to her soul and hypnotic until she heard a loud snorting sound and a dreadful stench filled her nostrils. Panic set in as she encountered a huge black bear staring at her from across the creek. Heart pounding, knees shaking, she backed up slowly and opened the car door. The bear was already lumbering across the water by the time she pulled the door shut. She turned the key, put the car in drive and took off. As she looked in her rear-view mirror, she could see the bear crossing the road. Her stomach was still clenched tight as she sped down the winding road. How fast she thought, life can shift from total tranquility to unnerving panic. The Army had trained her how to handle such situations when dealing with humans, but bears had not been in the training guide. Now that she was miles away from the massive beast, she could laugh out loud. Even if she didn't get the job, she would have quite the story to tell.

She pulled into the parking lot and before she put the car in park, she checked the address on her phone. There must be some mistake. She was expecting a hospital-like building, not a weathered wood framed garage. The number on her phone matched the painted number on the side of the building but she could not believe she was going for a job interview in this run-down structure. It looked to be in the same shape as the Corbin welcome sign she had seen along Route 1. She was determined to live a simpler life, but could she get used to living with poverty surrounding her?

She glazed her lips with a fresh coat of Pearl Pink, grabbed her briefcase from the front seat and opened the door to a new adventure. What she found inside caused her to take a breath of utter disbelief. It was like walking back in time: a time she never knew existed. As she took a quick visual sweep of the space, she noticed the few scattered rugs laying on the gray cement floor. The walls were merely plywood painted god-awful colors. A few crudely made cupboards had been nailed to the walls. Most had doors but some were open, displaying supplies kept in old coffee cans. A few beds with worn out bed sheets and blankets sat in the far corner.

A young lady sat on a metal folding chair behind a battered desk leafing through a stack of papers. The window curtains were tattered as if mice had wrestled with them for nesting material. Molly turned to walk back out the door when she noticed a small child lying on a cot behind a file cabinet. She was sleeping, but with labored breathing. An overall weighted feeling took hold of Molly and brought her focus back as to why she was here. These people needed help.

"Howdy, Ma'am, I'm sorry I didn't talk right away but I was counting, and I didn't want to lose my train of thought." She smiled mischievously, "I'm not really good with numbers. Is there something I can help you with?"

"Yes, my name is Molly Carlson. I had an appointment with Dr. Mitchell about the nursing position."

The young girl's eyebrows shot up in surprise. "Really? You really came? We were expecting you to call and say you couldn't make it. You're the first one who's ever showed up. Doc ain't here right now. Bessie Mae went into labor this morning and he rode up the mountain to look in on her."

Molly smiled, thinking how simple life must be around here. "Miss, can I ask why I'm the only one who came for an interview?"

The girl pressed her lips together as a sign of slight annoyance and spoke, "My name ain't Miss, it's Jolene. Just like the girl in Dolly Parton's song. You know that song?"

Molly fell instantly in love with this girl. She was so innocent. "Yes, I know that song and I love it, but you didn't answer my question."

Jolene brushed back some hair that had escaped from her ponytail and with her right hand gestured at their surroundings. "You really think anyone wants to work here?"

"But you're here," Molly said matter-of-factly.

She bent her head and studied her hands. "I was born here. It's my lot in life. When the doc offered me this job, I took it, knowing it was more opportunity than I deserve."

"Excuse me Jolene, but why would you say that?" You're a beautiful young lady and seem intelligent enough. You shouldn't put yourself down like that. Dr. Mitchell is lucky to have you."

"I do my best, but as you can see by the looks of this place there is so much that needs done."

Molly turned her attention to the sleeping child and asked, "What is wrong with her? Is she sick or just napping?"

"That's my daughter, Olivia. I have to bring her to work with me cause I can't afford a sitter. Doc's nice enough to let me do that. Speakin' of Doc, he just pulled in the parking lot. He'll be mighty glad to meet you." Then she added, "And surprised."

When the tall lean figure swaggered through the open doorway, Molly was too surprised to do more than nod. As their eyes met, she felt a shock run through her. His smile turned his mouth into the most beautiful set of teeth she had ever seen. "Good afternoon. May I help you?"

Jolene excitedly interrupted. "This is Molly. She came for the interview. She's a nurse."

"Well is that so?" With tanned, bare arms beneath rolled up shirtsleeves, he offered his hand and his name.

"Pleased to meet you Molly. I'm Dr. Dane Mitchell but everyone around here just calls me Doc. We're so glad you came. Let me show you around." With long, purposeful strides he walked through the building, explaining each box of supplies and reminding her of how solidly made the antiquated machines were.

Molly smiled, "These machines may be durable, but do they really do the job?"

"Well, Molly, here in Corbin any machine that helps us out medically is considered worthy."

Successfully disarming her with his smile, Molly felt a strange sense of confidence wash over her. This was exactly the kind of place crucial to her recovery. As much as she knew these people needed her, she was positive she needed them. The doctor was talking but she couldn't hear him. She was too absorbed in in her own thoughts. When he touched her shoulder, to get her attention, she was helpless to halt her embarrassment.

"I'm sorry, Dr. Mitchell, I didn't really hear what you were saying. I was thinking about how much I need this job." She continued in a much firmer voice, " I'm good at my job and I have quite a bit of experience. I may not be familiar with this particular kind of practice, but I have a lot compassion for people, which I'm assuming you need here."

Dr. Mitchell's eyes were shining with excitement. This girl had an air of calm and self-confidence he liked. Her resume' had been impressive enough and nursing the sick and wounded in a war zone was somewhat comparable to living in Corbin. Treating gunshot wounds was common.

"Molly, we would love to have you on board with us here if you're sure. Just know it takes a lot of courage and patience with the folk around here. They're a proud bunch of people and you must respect their culture. They'll give you the shirt off their back, but they want nothing for free."

Molly exchanged a smile with Doc and handed Jolene a paper with all her pertinent information.

"I have to give my two-week resignation at my current job and then I will return, ready to work. I am here for the weekend so could you direct me to a motel? I'm going to need an apartment when I move here, so I'll look around town for that today too."

Doc spoke up, "No need for that. The ad was supposed to say room and board included. Did it not say that?"

"Yes, actually it did but…"

The doctor interrupted, "But you're looking around here and afraid your accommodations might look like this. Am I right?"

Molly felt her cheeks burn with embarrassment, but before she found her voice, the doctor spoke, "I have a room over my garage that you're welcome to, if you'd like." He quickly added, "It's even furnished, and I think you'll like it."

Molly was shocked. This all seemed too good to be true. "That's very kind of you Dr. Mitchell. Could I see it today?"

"You can see it right now. I'll take you." He turned to Jolene, smiling and said, "You're in charge till I get back. I have my phone if it's an emergency. Let's go Molly, times a wastin'."

The apartment was beautiful and perfect for her. She wouldn't even have to worry about a moving van. Everything she needed from home would fit in her SUV. Dr. Mitchell, or Dane, as he insisted she call him, helped her bring the suitcase up the flight of steps into her new home.

She changed into jeans and returned to the clinic. She swept the cement. It had been a long time since she had seriously used a broom and she couldn't help laughing out loud. She finished cleaning the floor on the far side and arranged medical supplies, on the rickety shelves, in a more productive way. She understood why the place was in such disarray, being Jolene was swamped with paperwork and Dane was busy with patients. There was no one to take care of the basics. Cleaning was not what she was trained to do, but she would do what she had to, to make this a better place for the people of Boone County. Each sweep of the broom felt like it was pushing her one step closer to her purpose here on earth; something she was desperately searching for, something she knew she would find here.

Chapter 11

MAX

Max was in awe as he met one relative after another. There were so many, he wasn't sure how he would ever remember their names. His favorite so far was Aunt Alice, his mother's sister. She was an identical remake of his mother and he was having a hard time convincing himself this woman's name was Alice, not Isabella. She even had the soft sag beneath her chin. Alice's hair was simply washed and worn natural, while his mother preferred hair dark as coal. She wasn't tall, but like his mother, held herself like a queen. She had a quiet air of authority, and yet of rare warmth. The more he observed her, the more curious he got. How could two sisters, drift so far apart and lose all contact with each other. Once the reunion was over, he planned to do some investigating.

As Max intermingled with his newly found relatives, he discovered having a family was a whole lot different than he ever imagined. Seemed like everyone had a different opinion about everything. There were the paragons of upper society and then there were those of a more sensible, practical nature.

Uncle Don, a World War II veteran, was a man who craved the security of tradition. He had a masculine force about him, a great presence born of certainty, which he assumed gave him the right to expect America to uphold the Constitution and its values. He was always ready to protest the new generation and their prodigal ways.

"You boys go help your grandmother with the dishes."

"But Pops, we're boys. Dishes are supposed be washed by girls!"

"I help your grandmother do all kinds of "women's work." "So, are you saying I'm a girl?'

Both boys chimed in. "No, but you're old, so it doesn't matter!"

"Well, since I'm your "Pops" and I want you to grow up to be "real" men, I want you to go do that entire sink of dishes waiting to be washed. I also want you to dry them and put them away."

"But Pop's!"

"Don 't "Pops" me. You need to understand how important it is to help each other. Doesn't matter if it's a man or woman. A person needs help, you help them." Uncle Don rubbed the tense muscles in the back of his neck. "You're telling me if someone knocks into a girl at school would you just stand there and let her be hurt?"

The youngest of the cousins answered first, "No, unless the guy was bigger than me."

"Young man, I fought in a war where every guy was bigger than me. I fought for your freedom so you could have the opportunity and the desire to help each other, no matter the gender." The old man held the young boy's eyes with mesmerizing force as he spoke, "I know you boys have good hearts. They run in the family." He waved his hand in a gesture of dismissal. "Now go use them!"

Max had been mixing with the relatives, trying to figure out which one would give him a true account of his mother before she hauled him away to Willow Grove. What had been her reason for not allowing him to be a part of this quirky, yet caring family?

Just now, listening to Uncle Don reprimand his grandsons gave Max an inside glimpse to the man he knew he would be proud to call Uncle. He recognized a man, proud of his country and not afraid to defend his freedom. Hopefully the boys had enough respect for their grandfather to take his words to heart. Max was convinced Uncle Don knew the most and would tell him the story of his mother, Isabella, with candor and loyalty. But for now, Max was content to enjoy his new-found family.

"Max, come fill your plate!" Max loved hearing those words. His mother had never been a very good cook and most things he ate during childhood came out of a box. How could two women with the same blood coursing through their veins, be so different; Aunt Alice, who seemed to bring people together with her flair for feeding the masses, and his mother, who hated being in the kitchen and didn't like crowds. He was so eager to find all the answers, but he knew he had to wait for the right opportunity.

For now, he would answer the call from his stomach and make Aunt Alice happy.

Chapter 12

Molly

Molly stood in complete surprise when she opened the door to the breakroom in the hospital. Her feelings took over the moment, breathing an almost exaggerated humility. She had tried to be a great supervisor to her nursing staff, but she always worried about what they might have said behind her back. Seeing everyone gathered here gave here new perspectives on that thought. Even some doctors who had not always agreed with her techniques, had taken time to come say good bye. Dr. McCoy, Chief of Staff whistled, to get everyone's attention and raised his glass of punch high in the air. "Molly Carlson, we want you to know that you are going to be missed." He grinned, to put her at ease. "As you know, we didn't always see eye-to-eye, but you weren't afraid of me, and for that, I commend you. You're a hell of a nurse Molly. We wish you luck in your new adventure." He stepped forward and gave her a friendly hug. She looked up, flashing a smile of thanks.

Dr. McCoy's booming voice ricocheted off the walls as he announced break-time was over. With tears and hugs, one by one, her colleagues said goodbye and wished her luck.

Standing alone in a room filled with friends made her question her decision to move to an impoverished part of the country. What made her think she would find what she was looking for among people of a different culture. Did she have something she could share with them or was she hoping they would share their humble and simple ways with her? Could she live without the conveniences of the modern world? From the minute she drove into Corbin, she felt drawn to the modesty of the area. She was tired of the hustle-bustle of the city and the stress her PTSD laid upon her. It was time to unload that part of her life and start over. She felt the only way to do that would be new surroundings.

She returned to her office with an empty box and filled it with the few mementos she had kept on her desk. She turned off the computer, said goodbye one more time and walked out the door, leaving a part of herself behind.

Loading her car was more of a challenge than she anticipated, and she was glad when she was able to forcibly shut the trunk.

The splendor of bold mountains and sparkling streams became consistent as Molly drove south to her new destination. Between the canopy of trees, she caught glimpses of swanlike clouds drifting in the clear sky, high above the peaks. She passed farmhouses set in deep lush valleys, surrounded by fence posts and barbed wire. She appreciated the seeds, blown by the wind and scattered among the roadside grasses. They had added bright spots of color to this rural countryside.

She had debated as to whether she should return to Corbin by the same road she had encountered the bear, or travel on the interstate, sure to be free of wild animals.

She chose the now familiar route along the creek. Bear or no bear, she found peace as she drove through the beautiful countryside. Serenity surrounded her, influencing her mood as she drove into a new chapter of life.

Molly followed the directions given to her by the doctor, guiding her to the front door of her new apartment. Even though it was over a garage it had a cottage-type feel to it and she loved it. It was bright with lots of windows and the gleaming wood floors were polished to a high shine. The bedroom walls, covered in softly striped wallpaper, along with an iron bed and a modern dresser, gave the room a warm feeling. A small sunroom, off the kitchen, created the perfect spot for a small round table. A beautiful vase full of fresh flowers sat in the middle on a hand-made crocheted doily. The flowers brought the entire room alive with their scent. Seemed like the doctor had thought of everything!

Molly unpacked her clothes, some personal items and some food. She had planned to make a grocery run but it looked like the doctor had beat her to it. The cupboards were full. And the items were things on her grocery list. How did he know what to buy? She made a mental note to ask him that question when she felt a little more comfortable around him.

She locked the door and drove towards the clinic. When she arrived, three people were sitting on folding chairs outside waiting for the doctor.

"Hi! My name's Molly. I'm the new nurse here. Are you waiting for someone?"

Molly | 63

Cold and steady as a stone, the old man answered, "Yea, we's here to see the doc."

"Does Jolene know you're here?"

He smiled, but it was without humor, "You's think just cuz you got some education that makes you smarter than us? We ain't sittin here for fun. It's too hot ta sit inside."

The old man looked at her with a sardonic expression that sent Molly's temper soaring and she reacted angrily to the challenge in his voice. Was this how everyone would treat her, she wondered? She swallowed hard, trying not to reveal her anger as she answered him." I'm sorry sir, this is my first day here and I guess I'm a bit nervous. I did not mean to offend you. I am coming to work for Dr. Mitchell, and I have yet to learn your ways. I hope your wait won't be long." She forced a smile and went inside. She soon understood why outside was better. It was stifling hot in the building, even with a huge fan running.

Jolene looked up from her paperwork and pleasantly said, "Good afternoon, Molly. I'm glad you had a safe trip. Doc is in that little room over there, if you'd like to go in. He's waitin' on ya!"

Molly knocked lightly before opening the door only to find the doctor in the arms of a lady, old enough to be his mother. He made no apologies, as he loosened his grip. "Good afternoon Molly, let me introduce you to Nellie Parker. She is the Doyenne of the mountain".

"Please to meet you Nellie. I'm not sure what Doyenne means but I'd guess it means a beautiful lady!"

"Nellie shot the doc a gracious wink and in a smooth, dark old voice she said, "Honey that's awful kind of you to say that, but doyenne means mostly that people around here highly respect me for my cookin' skills. I can take a side of bear meat and cook it so's it'll melt in your mouth. You bring me meat, or any vegetable and I'll give those high-paid people on TV a run for their money." She stared at Molly with smoldering intensity. "Do you cook young lady?"

"I'm not much of a cook, no, I seem to be too busy to learn."

Nellie got in the doctor's face and spoke a little louder, "You bring this youngin' to me and I'll show her what real cookin' is!"

Doc laughed warmly and richly. "I'll do that Nellie, now you make sure you get some rest and take the medicine Jolene is going to give you. She'll have the directions written down for you. You take care now and I'll see you back here in two weeks. In the meantime, if you need anything, you call me." He leaned down and kissed her on her leathery cheek and helped her out of the room.

Molly never felt such primal attraction to any male before, except the medical salesman back in Willow Grove. He was more the knight-in-shining armor type, where, as this guy was genuinely kind, even to old ladies. He seemed to be the real thing.

Jolene interrupted Molly's musings with "Naomi and Clayton are waiting outside with their son. He has another bad cold and they've brought him in for a breathing treatment."

"Okay Jolene, I'll bring them in." Molly opened the door and spoke simply. "Naomi and Clayton, the doctor is ready to see your son now." Naomi's grin widened, only to show a few surviving teeth, but she stood and patiently helped her son get on his feet. His features carried a startling load of information. Molly mentally diagnosed him with minimal cystic fibrosis. No wonder he constantly needed breathing treatments. With more compassion now, she went to his side, took him by the arm and assisted him into the clinic. Once inside, the doctor began the treatment with the nebulizer until Jacob's lungs were clear.

No sooner had Naomi and Layton left, until a tiny sprite of a woman came through the front door. The first thing Molly noticed was pink plastic curlers wound tight and in no order, around silvery locks of hair. She smiled as she remembered when her mother had worn them to bed every night.

"Molly, this is Ruby, and she comes here once a week so we can take her blood pressure. Would you please do that for her today?"

"Sure thing Jolene." Molly reached for the cuff and put it gently on the frail arm. " Pleased to meet you Ruby. My name is Molly and I guess we'll be seeing a lot of each other from now on." This dear woman was what Molly had envisioned as a "hill person." Her mental vocabulary was very limited and when she spoke, it was in an agonized whisper that tore at Molly's heart.

The remainder of the day continued with a constant flow of patients. Molly was exhausted and fell into bed still dressed in scrubs.

Chapter 13

MOLLY

Molly was eating her last bite of cereal when the phone rang. "Is this Nurse Molly?" She almost choked. No one had called her that since Afghanistan.

"Yes, this is she. Who am I speaking to?"

She heard his voice, chuckling and hearty, "Still prim and proper huh? Would you like me to sing you a country song?"

"General Patton!" Molly couldn't believe she was hearing his voice. "How are you and where are you?"

"I'm good. I got a couple of new prosthetics and hearing aids so I'm as normal as I'm ever going to be. I moved back to my hometown in Iowa and I'm enjoying life. How bout you? You're still a nurse I hope, cause you were a damn good one."

"Thank you, sir."

"I was so shocked when I heard your voice on the answering machine. You said you needed a favor. I hope you're alright."

"I'm fine, and to answer your question, yes I'm still a nurse. I recently moved to Kentucky and I work with a doctor in the Appalachian Mountains. I think I'm going to find it very rewarding. But the reason I called you is because I need help with something else."

The General interjected, "You just name it and I'll do whatever I can."

Molly continued, "When I returned home from the Army, there was a man who died in our town. He had been a burn victim, so he had no fingerprints, and no one seemed to know him or care about him. Anyhow, I was snowmobiling through the cemetery when I found fresh footprints in the snow that led to his gravesite. I can't quit wondering who would be visiting him if no one knew who he was. I seemed to have the feeling that he was a former soldier. And the reason being, I found a necklace laying in the snow, as if someone had brought that instead of flowers. I found out it's an ancient Middle Eastern charm symbolizing the Hand of God. People believe it will protect them from evil forces. It's supposed to bring its owner good fortune. It's called a Hamsa and it's shaped like a hand."

General Patton interrupted again, "I saw quite a few of them in Afghanistan. They were very popular with the Afghanistan soldiers. A lot of American GI's wore them too."

"I thought too it looked familiar, so my gut tells me that John Doe must have been a soldier. He must have a family somewhere wondering what happened to him and I'd like to be able to bring them closure. That's where you come in."

"What can I do?"

"Do you still know anyone who could get names of burn victims who served overseas and where they were sent for treatment, how long they were there, that sort of thing?'

The General spoke in his casual, jesting way, "I do still have a few connections. I'll get on it right away. I'll call you the minute I know something." He hesitated and then his voice dropped in volume, "Thanks for calling Molly. I needed an assignment. I'll do my best."

"Thank you, sir."

Chapter 14

MAX

Max's gentle nudge on his uncle's shoulder wakened him from his nap on the rocking chair. "Didn't get enough sleep last night Uncle Don? I thought you were sitting here reading the paper."

"I was, a few minutes ago. Must've dozed off."

Max nodded and smiled, indicating he understood.

"You look like you got somethin' on your mind." Uncle Don peered out over his reading glasses and questioned, "Anything I can do to help?"

Max sounded anxious with need, "I hope so. I have so many questions about my mother."

Uncle Don knew he had the power to wound this young man with negative words, but what good could come of that. Everyone who met Max had presented themselves as being happy to meet him, as they should have when meeting a long-lost relative. After all, it wasn't Max's fault. He had been a baby when his mother had removed him from the family.

Max, sitting on the edge of the sofa, waiting for an answer, looked so much like his alleged father, Silas

Cooper. Twenty-eight years ago, when Silas was a sailor in the Navy, it was rumored that he and Isabella were lovers. There had been no proof, but since meeting Max, Don had no doubt it was true. He was physically a clone of his father, but he was over-flowing with his mother's mannerisms. He was quiet and deep but with an inbred force of strength, something the "hill people" were born with.

He looked directly at Max and said, "I'm not sure how many of your questions I can answer, but I'll do my best. Being raised in these mountains, even when you don't have much money, can be a wonderful way of life, if you are lucky enough to have two god-fearing parents, but if your old man is a moonshiner and your mother is treated like a door-mat, your chances of breaking that cycle are less than zero."

"Is that how my mother and Aunt Alice were raised? How did they get out?"

"Your Aunt Alice was only ten when your grandfather died, so she didn't have to live her teenage years under his regime. Your grandfather didn't have much time for his children until they were older and of some use to him. He thought it was woman's work to do all the coddlin', as he called it, and when they were strong enough to do his chores, he used them like mule horses." Uncle Don leaned back against the rocking chair, fell silent for a few minutes and without warning gave a non-committal grunt."

Max reacted by flinching.

"Sorry Max, didn't mean ta scare ya. Talkin about all this is bringin back some of my own memories."

"I'm sorry Uncle Don. We don't have to do this now. I just thought out of everyone I've met; you would be the best one to tell the story. I feel as though I can trust you to tell the truth."

"Thank ya son. I appreciate that. Like I said, I'll tell ya what I know. I just haven't thought about this stuff for a long time and my childhood days were pretty much like your mother's. And truth be known, most everyone else who lived on this mountain have the same recollections. So, our generation has tried to break the cycle. Moonshinin' is still an occupation but the threat of getting caught is so much greater than it used to be, so it's not worth the risk nowadays, especially if your trying to raise a family." He looked at Max and got a little closer. "Men your age now have some education and can get a decent salary if they are willing to step off the mountain and work for someone else. Back in my day you were considered a traitor to these hills if you did that." He provided a sheepish grin as he winked, "Women are even working away from the home now."

Max got the feeling he had opened a can of worms with his uncle, by inquiring about his mother when he saw the drops of moisture clinging to his shiny bald head. "It's okay, Uncle Don, you don't have to continue this if it's making you uncomfortable."

Leaning forward in his chair, he continued as though Max had never spoken. "If you were born a female in these mountains it was just a fact that you took care of your siblings, the gardening, the canning, everything associated with the inside of the house. If you were born a male you worked with your dad outside, even at the still. From the time you could keep up in the woods, the boys shadowed the father and most of them continued in his footsteps. When the girls reached thirteen, they not only had to continue their work in the house, but they were also expected to help with the moonshine. It was hard work and they had to do it in all kinds of weather. Being plum worn-out, some caught colds, which turned into pneumonia and they died. The strong ones found other ways to survive. Your mother was one of the resilient ones. She got married at the age of fourteen, to get out from under her father's demands. But she stepped right out of the fryin pan into the fire. Her husband turned out to be worse than her father. But there were no divorces in these hills at that time. You stuck it out until one of ya's was dead."

Max interrupted again, "My mother obviously lived, so does that mean my father died and that's why she left Corbin?"

Uncle Don shifted uneasily, not sure how to answer. Should he echo the long-ago rumors or send him to someone who would tell the real story. But who would that be? There had been a real scandal, and rumors had flown every which way. Some said that only three people knew the truth. Since Isabella's death, that left two. The Sheriff and his deputy, Diggor.

"Max, I said I would tell you what I know, and I've done that. I don't want to repeat the gossip that occupied this town for years. Your mother's family was well-known in these parts and your grandfather was a high-ranking member of " The Mountain Mafia."

Max's words had bite – "I come from Mafia?" He repeated the words, this time louder. Is that really the truth?"

Uncle Don had no intention of letting Max think the worst of the hill folk. "Now don't get your britches in an uproar. The Mafia back then was not like the Mafia of today. The townspeople, who had nothing to do with moonshine, gave the well-known bootleggers this title. It was easier to group them all together and call them Mafia than to name them individually. They did not enjoy a comfortable life. They worked hard at their trade. Most of their time was spent staying one foot ahead of the revenuers, so they had little time to experience life, as we know it."

Charlie came into the room whining and scratching at Max's leg. Max patted him on the head and told him he would have to wait.

Uncle Don gestured with his head towards the door. "Take him outside Max. No sense punishing the dog because of history. Basically, I've told you all I know. I loved your mother simply because Alice loved her and looked up to her. Deciding to leave her home was one thing, but severing herself from the family caused a lot of pain to your aunt. She has always blamed herself for your mother's leaving. She convinced herself she could've done more to persuade her sister to stay."

Max had felt an instant connection to his uncle and after listening to him he understood why. He was likable and competent. He seemed to have incredible energy and Max got the feeling he was the cornerstone of the family. Without him there may not have been relatives for Max to reunite with.

"Thanks, Uncle Don. I appreciate your time. If it weren't for me, maybe my mother would never have left the mountain."

"Don't let that worry you son, cause I can tell you for a fact, your mother was going to find a way out of the mountain, with or without you. You were her pride and joy and she just wanted the best for you. Someday maybe we'll all find out the whole story. Until then, we're glad you came to visit. It's been nice having you here and we'll miss you when you go. Go now and take care of that dog!"

Chapter 15

MOLLY

Molly had enjoyed her weekend, just driving in and around town, familiarizing herself with streets and restaurants. According to signs all over town, Corbin was "Home of the Moonbow." Curiosity aroused, she found the library and did some research on this phenomenon. It was something she had never heard of before, but it was a real spectacle in this town and visitors from all over came to see the display. Moonbows occur at night when there is a full moon and if tonight's moon would be in harmony with last night, she would be able to witness this marvel. The river wasn't far from town and she planned to see this for herself.

She found an empty bench in the park to eat her Texas-style hot dog and a bag of chips. Focused on inserting the straw into the super-sized Coke, she swung her head around to see who had put their hand on her shoulder and lost control of the cup. The dark liquid splattered all over her, the bench and onto the ground.

"I'm so sorry Molly. I didn't mean to startle you."

When Molly recognized the voice, a cry of relief broke from her lips. She thought a stranger was trying to approach her. "Dr. Mitchell! I'm so glad it's you. I was thinking the worst."

"I should know better than to walk up behind you." He reached for the empty cup and said, "Let me get you another drink."

"No, I'm fine. I'm almost finished with my gourmet meal anyhow, so I don' t need the coke. I'll get one later." She gestured in a sweeping motion with one arm, "This is a beautiful park. I was just out exploring when I found it. It's very relaxing here."

The doctor felt his cheeks burn with embarrassment. "Well it was, till I made you spill your drink."

He picked up the empty cup and threw it in the trash can. "If you're up to it, I'll show you some of the historical landmarks around here. Have you heard of the Moonbow?"

"I have. I'm planning on going there tonight."

"If it's alright, I'd be glad to be your guide! It's really an amazing opportunity. And the falls are spectacular. We could grab a bite to eat later, and then go on over to the falls and wait for the night show."

"That would be great, but I don't want to inconvenience you. I'm sure you have things you need to do."

It had been a long time since Dane had been with a woman. Commitment to his work and to the people who needed his help had forced him to put his own needs aside. But now those forgotten desires were being awakened by this woman standing in front of him. She was dressed in khaki shorts and a baggy t-shirt, making no effort at all to be sexy, yet her femininity was not lessened by her choice of clothing. She had, what Dane would call, a gentle and overwhelming beauty. Since the first time he met her he had been imagining himself softly brushing a tendril of hair away from her face, giving him a chance to claim her lips.

"Dr. Mitchell? Obviously, you have a lot of things on your mind. I don't think you heard me. I said you don't have to feel obligated to show me around."

Dane considered himself a level-headed man and standing here acting like a love-sick puppy was not being very professional. The awkward moment between them passed and he spoke. "If we don't see the Moonbow tonight we'll have to wait another month. It's only visible during full moon so I'll pick you up at seven o'clock, we'll grab a burger and then drive to the falls. Bring a jacket, it gets cool in the evening by the water."

"I'll be ready. I'm looking forward to it."

She watched as he walked away, convincing herself that her attraction to him was a purely physical thing. She had only been working with him for a week, but she had to admit, within those few days she had found him to be self-confident, shadowed by genuine kindness. It was easy to work beside him. Even though he was the doctor, he was not the least bit intimidating. Molly smiled as she thought about spending the evening with her boss.

True to his word, the doctor rang her doorbell at seven o'clock. Molly grabbed her jacket and opened the door. Dane was dressed in jeans and a polo-shirt, not what she was used to seeing on the doctors at Willow Grove. They had a dress code of khaki pants, shirt and tie. Even after work, they seemed to continue their same attire. Dane wore scrubs to work. Said it made laundry easy and in the morning, he didn't have to think about what to wear. Molly had initially found him to have this naturally captivating presence, even in scrubs. But now, dressed so casually, she was even more rivetted. She could see that his backside filled out the Levi's to perfection. She also couldn't help noticing the bits of brown curly hair poking out through the top opening of his shirt.

"Dr. Mitchell, right on time."

A lighthearted smile creased his lips, "Please call me Dane, when we're not at the office."

She returned the smile and offered her hand. "It's a deal, Dane!"

Dane chuckled as he watched Molly devour the cheeseburger, along with a large order of fries.

"Was I right when I said these were the best burgers in town?"

Mouth full, Molly tried to answer, "Yes, you were so right. I'm sorry, I must be acting like a pig, but that hotdog this afternoon just didn't do it for me. I didn't realize I was this hungry."

"Glad I could come to your rescue. As a doctor, it's a pleasure to see someone with a great appetite. It's characteristic of a healthy individual."

Molly was fascinated as she focused on Dane's explanation of what he hoped she would witness later in the evening. "A moonbow is a rainbow produced by moonlight rather than direct sunlight. Its formation is the same as a rainbow; the only difference is the light source. It's caused by the refraction of light in many water droplets, such as the waterfalls and is always positioned in the opposite part of the sky from the moon, relative to the observer." Dane winked and said, "Are you getting all of this?"

Molly only nodded her head, afraid if she talked, her memory would fail her. Dane continued, as if he were the teacher and she the student. "Moonbows are much paler than rainbows due to the smaller amount of light reflected from the surface of the moon. Typically, it is too weak for the human eye to discern color, so we usually only see white." He quickly added, "However, color does appear in some long exposure photographs."

He walked closer to the railing and resumed the description. "Moonbows are easier to see when the moon is at its brightest phrase, or what we call "full moon'. We're lucky tonight. There is no cloud cover."

He turned his face to the sky and proudly said, "There are only three places in the United States that Moonbows occur and we're lucky enough to be one of those places." He moved closer to Molly and continued talking, "Even if there was no Moonbow, I would still choose to live in Corbin. It's a great little town."

"Have you always lived here?"

"All my life, except for my years away at college. I've always wanted to be a doctor and I've always wanted to come back here. My grandparents were 'hill people' and they never had adequate health care. I watched them both suffer from illnesses that could have been prevented, if they would have had the right care and guidance. When I was sixteen, I made a promise to God – let me ace medical school and I will dedicate my life and my medical skills to helping the less fortunate. God kept his end of the bargain so now I'm keeping mine."

"You really believe that don't you?"

Her scrutiny made him uncomfortable. "Well of course, I believe that, don't you?" Have you never made a deal with God?"

"Can't say that I have. I'm not even sure I believe in God."

Dane closed his eyes and took a deep breath, "Molly, I'm going to let you in on a little secret. The people around here are God-fearing folks. They might have a lot of superstitions, but their faith outweighs any old-time myths. You might change your mind about God once you get to know the locals. They have enough faith to move these mountains anywhere they want them. Just listen and learn. These old-timers especially, have a lot of wisdom and they're willing to share. Once you get to know some of these folks, I hope some of your doubts will be alleviated."

While some of her troubled spirits and questions remained quiet, she struggled with underlying concepts about religion. She had been raised in a religious-free atmosphere. Her knowledge of Bible stories was limited to those she had heard in Bible School. She had memorized a few verses back then, but they were long gone in her memory bank. As a teenager, she had never acquired a liking to the party life or to dating so her diary was boring. Her parents were very strict and kept her busy with chores. Signing up for the military, without her parent's knowledge, was the most adventurous risk she had ever taken. And it turned out to be her saving grace. It's where she revealed her passion for nursing and where she found her purpose in life.

"Molly? It seems like I've touched on a sensitive area. I didn't mean to invade your private space, but I just wanted to prepare you for some of the upcoming conversations you might find yourself immersed in."

The doctor's concern for her was sweet but he didn't need to worry. She would not allow herself to become involved in religious conversations. "Thanks Dane, I'll take it under advisement. I appreciate your concern."

"He smiled and turned his attention back to the moonbow. The last rays of the sunset were fading to a deep navy blue. Molly retrieved her camera from her backpack, and they waited silently, as the silvery moonlight glimmered across the surface of the water beneath the falls. And then she saw it. The arch shaped bow was very faint at first, a shade of white that progressed into touches of color. It was breathtaking as she watched the transformation. She felt privileged to be seeing such an awesome sight.

When Dane brought her back home and pulled into the driveway, Molly thanked him and was out of the car before he had a chance to be a gentleman and open her door. "See you Monday morning. I really had a nice time tonight. Thanks again." She waved and disappeared through her front door. On the other side, she leaned back, reliving the evening. Did she want a relationship with her boss? He was easy on the eyes and he was a super nice guy. Kind, generous, everything she thought she wanted in a guy, she saw in Dane. There was an unspoken rule in the world of medical careers, especially among nurses; no matter how good looking or nice the doctor appeared to be, it was not a good idea to get hung up on your boss. It just never seemed to work out. This atmosphere differed greatly from the big-city hospitals and large medical practices, but red flags were still waving in front of her face.

    Molly found herself in the kitchen heating the tea kettle for a cup of chamomile tea. She hoped it would calm the many thoughts swirling around in her head, allowing her to get a good night's rest.

Chapter 16

MAX

Max stuffed the last of his shirts into the suitcase, pulled out the handle and moved toward the front door. He had said his goodbyes to everyone except Uncle Don and Aunt Alice. As he rolled the suitcase down the driveway, he popped the trunk open with the remote and called for Charlie. He opened the front door and the dog jumped in, eager to ride.

Aunt Alice came out of the house waving a brown paper bag, "I packed you a sandwich and a few snacks for your trip." She whispered, "There's some for Charlie too."

"Aunt Alice, you are aware Charlie doesn't know the whole English language, right?" She playfully slapped him on the arm and burst out laughing. "Of course, I do silly, but just in case, I wanted him to have a surprise! We're gonna miss the little guy. Oh, and we're gonna miss you too. When are you coming back?"

"I'm not sure. My business is new, so I spend a lot of time at work and I'm on the road quite a bit too. Being in sales requires a huge time commitment. As soon as I get a break, I'll come for another visit. It's been so much fun to meet everyone and see where I come from." He drew Aunt Alice into his arms, kissed her on the cheek and whispered, "Thank you." He held out an open hand to Uncle Don and with enthusiasm, repeated his appreciation.

He watched in his rear-view mirror as his newfound relatives stood waving in the driveway. He rubbed Charlie's head and said out loud, "We're not giving up, my friend. We are going to find out why my mother denied me the opportunity to belong to this fun-loving family." Charlie raised his head to acknowledge he was listening as Max continued. "Now mind you, I'm not saying I didn't have a good life, but it could have been ten times more fun with all those relatives. Just think about Christmas, Charlie. Think of all the people we could have celebrated with. And family reunions. Playing games with all my cousins! I just can't believe my mother, who swore she loved me, would deny me the privilege of knowing all these people. For twenty-four years she pushed the subject under the rug and kept it there. Whatever happened to cause such an abyss in the family without anyone knowing except my mother?" He ruffled Charlie's hair again and echoed his earlier statement. "We are not giving up Charlie."

Max returned to work early Monday morning, eager to hear his partners' version of his meeting with Molly Carlson. He poured himself a cup of coffee, hoping to calm his nerves before commiserating with Wayne. He was expecting him to have an exaggerated reason why Ms. Carlson would not approve the medical supply order.

"Before we get into the reason why you didn't get the account, tell me, what is your assessment of Molly Carlson?"

"Who?"

"Molly Carlson, the Director of Nurses, the one I told you that was sporting an attitude."

"Never met a Molly. The gal I met with was Lori and we got the account. It's even bigger than what you were expecting."

Max's mouth gaped open in surprise. "What happened to Molly?"

Wayne responded matter-of-factly, "She quit!"

Max tried to force his confused emotions into order. He was glad he wouldn't have to deal with her anymore but he was looking forward to seeing her again. Why would she quit a job she was obviously good at? "Do you know any details, my friend?"

"I went to the hospital and spoke to the lady at the front desk. When I said I had an appointment with Ms. Carlson, she stated that Ms. Carlson no longer worked at the hospital and that I would now be working with Lori, the new Director of Nurses. You know me, I thought Ms. Carlson might have died or something, so I just came out and asked if she was still alive. The old lady behind the desk had eyes that could carve a man to pieces without even trying. She very strongly told me that the nurse in question had moved to Kentucky and that was all I needed to know. I tipped my imaginary hat and found my way to the new director's office." Wayne leaned back in his chair and flashed a good-humored smile. "I think you'll like working with Lori. I found her to have no attitude towards our supplies. She was very nice!"

Max took Wayne's ribbing in stride. He tried to be funny in everything he did, but today, it wasn't working.

He kept asking himself two questions; why Molly would quit, and where did she go. Kentucky was a big state with many people. How would he ever find her? And did he want to find her? His head was saying forget about her, but his heart wasn't agreeing.

Max threw himself into his work and months passed. He handled the hospital account, and Wayne was right, Lori was nice and easy to work with. So why was he missing the red-headed girl with attitude? He was having dreams of brushing her deep auburn hair away from her face, kissing her lightly, but lingering. He felt as though he had missed an opportunity to make her fall in love with him. Thoughts of her were affecting his work. He couldn't concentrate. Everywhere he looked, something reminded him of Molly. But why? He barely knew her and yet, he felt destined to be with her.

Nightmares of Afghanistan had returned, and persistent leg cramps were causing restless nights for Max. Shadows deepened under his eyes. His whole body was engulfed in tides of weariness and despair.

"Max, you look like hell. Are you sick and not telling me?" Wayne sat down on the corner of the big desk and waited for an answer.

"No Wayne, I'm not sick. I've been having nightmares again and I can't sleep. Some nights I can't breathe. It's as if the air in my house is thick with dust. I hear guns and people moaning. Then my leg starts cramping and I'm right back in Afghanistan, crouching in the corner, not being able to reach my men."

Wayne didn't move nor speak. He thought it was good for Max to say this stuff out loud. He had never been a soldier, so he had no idea what Max, or millions of others had gone through, but if listening helped, then he would sit here for as long as Max needed to talk.

Max's voice cracked with anger and humiliation, "I can't stop the rage that knots my gut every time I think about my men and how I didn't protect them. I had run ahead to inspect the building and found it empty, so I radioed for my men to follow when a grenade exploded, killing two and wounding three. I caught some shrapnel, causing my right arm to be useless, and my left too weak to shoulder my weapon. I suffered a concussion as well and then spent most of my time in the field hospital, unconscious. The physical pain was nothing compared to the emotional torture."

Wayne could see his friend was carrying a heavy burden on his shoulders, but he had no idea how to help.

Max lowered his voice to an intimate whisper, "I truly believe that a soldier who has participated in war may be able to reclaim his physical body, but emotionally, the war for him, always exists. I have been fortunate to be able to go to therapy, and I'll be the first to admit that it did help, and I've also been lucky that my body has responded well to the medicine. What I don't understand is what's triggered this anxiety now? Whatever it is, I need to find a way to resolve it."

Wayne stayed silent, giving Max time to pull himself together. He tried, but when he talked again, his voice broke with emotion. "I'm sorry Wayne. My therapist is the only one who has ever seen me in this state and I'm not sure what's caused these memories to flare up again, but I can't let them go on any longer. I hate to do this to you again, but can you handle things here? If you need to hire someone, do it. I have enough money saved to hold me for a while. I think I need a sabbatical."

Wayne was shocked. "Where and what are you going to do?"

Passion thickened Max's voice as he spoke, "I'm not sure, but my first thought is to go back to my roots in Kentucky. I felt like I belonged there, something I've never felt before." He ramped up the volume as he continued, "I promise I'll keep in touch and I hope to be back soon. You know this business better than me anyhow, so you'll do fine. I have a lot of faith in you, Wayne. I know you'll make it work." Max found a box, filled it with the few personal items he had on his desk and carried them to his car.

He sat behind the steering wheel cradling his pounding head in his hands, wondering if he had allowed his emotions to cloud his judgment. He had just quit his job. What was he going to do for an income? Luckily, he had inherited the house from his mother, with no debt, but he still needed money to maintain the premises. His head hurt from all the confusing thoughts and they were making him doubt himself. He should go home and talk it over with Charlie. Sometimes, vocally expressing his thoughts to the dog helped put them into perspective.

Max woke up the next morning feeling better than he had in a long time. Afghanistan had not haunted him during the night, except for the image of a red-headed nurse. It was a far stretch from his usual nightmares. He remembered nothing about his time spent in the field hospital. He had been unconscious most of the time and when he finally woke up, he was told of his unit's casualties. More than he could deal with, he fell into a state of depression. He exaggerated his pain in exchange for morphine. He wanted no part of the existing world but the Army anticipated a full recovery, so he was soon sent back out on a reconnaissance mission.

Max packed his suitcase while he waited for his coffee to brew. He then washed out his travelling cup, eager for his morning caffeine. He brought the cooler in from the garage and emptied the fridge of anything that might spoil. Charlie was already sitting by his blanket as a reminder it dare not be left behind. Max carried the blanket, toys and a bag of dog food to the car. He loaded the remainder of his things in the trunk and found Charlie already comfortable in the front seat.

Max laughed out loud as he acknowledged the ball of fur on the seat, "I guess I don't have to ask you twice, do I? He plugged the GPS system into the cigarette lighter, turned on the ignition and prayed this journey would come to pass as the beginning of the rest of his life.

Chapter 17

MAX

Max pulled his car into Alice and Tom's driveway, excited to see them again. He was happy to see Bruce already on the front porch. Charlie was standing, looking out the car window, eager to run in the front yard.

"Good to see you again cuz. I can't believe you're thinking of moving here. We just got an opening on the local baseball team. Interested? I bet you're a home-run hitter, aren't you?"

"Slow down there Bruce. One question at a time. I am interested in playing ball and yes, I've hit my share of home-runs."

Bruce's head bobbed in agreement. "I knew it." Gesturing toward Max's shoulders, he continued. " With arms like that I bet people in the next county can hear the smack when bat meets ball."

"Well, I think you're exaggerating a bit, but I might allow you to persuade me to try out."

"Tomorrow then. Be ready by six. We play on the high-school field." Deserting the subject of baseball, he steered the conversation toward Max's trip. His smile turned to a chuckle as he asked, "Didn't have any deer trying to get in your car this time, did you? "

"No, I had a big sign made for on the side of my car that said, "No Deer Allowed!"

Bruce continued laughing and came back with "Good one, Max, good one."

Max spent the next few weeks looking for an apartment and a job. Uncle Don sent him to Best Medical Supply, in Somerset, the neighboring town. Mr. Baker, the owner, hired him on the spot. "Your resume` looks great and I'll be proud to hire any relative of Don Watkins. He and I go back a long way. Your timing couldn't be better. My top salesman just retired last week."

Max thanked him with an enthusiastic handshake and followed him down the hall to view his newly assigned office, complete with a huge bay window. Greenery from the hanging plants was tangled with foliage planted in the pots on the wide oak sill. It was a jungle and Max made a mental note to bring a watering can and come to the aid of these water-deprived plants.

Max's creative personality and experience in the field of medical supplies harmonized well with the other employees. He had an incredible energy behind his skills and people seemed to gravitate towards him, respecting his opinion. He wasn't menacing but he was sure of himself when marketing was involved. The most amazing feeling had come over him since living here in Corbin; it felt like he had lived here all his life. This deep-gut feeling of belonging, of being where he was meant to be, was incredible. It was a new emotion for him, and he was humbled by it.

The ad in the paper said, "Apartment for rent. One bedroom, one bath. Immediate occupancy." Max called and set up an appointment directly after work. It was just his style, that bit of modern, yet homey character. The owners fell in love with Charlie and agreed he would be welcome. Max signed the lease and was handed the key.

Don and Bruce assured Max they would empty out the storage unit he had been renting and deliver his belongings to his new home. Just as they promised, Max opened his front door to find boxes piled high in his living room. Charlie had made himself at home on his blanket, near the kitchen.

The apartment was feeling like home to both Max and Charlie. The anxiety that had spurted through Max initially, seemed less and less each evening as he watched the sun set and disappear behind the mountains. He convinced himself that he had been here long enough for people to get used to his presence and for him to earn peoples trust. His initial reason for the upheaval in his life was to understand his mother's reasoning for the path she had embraced. He wanted to know his family and his roots. He wanted to belong, and where else to satisfy that desire, than in the town where he was conceived and born.

He had asked older people around town had they known his mother and the response he got was always the same. They would stare at him as if they were looking at a ghost, mumble something unintelligible and simply walk away. He had tried to start a conversation with his co-workers about the Mountain Mafia, but they sincerely were clueless. He went to the library, hoping to find newspaper articles relating to his mother or anyone in her family, but found nothing. He hoped to probe further into Uncle Don's memory and bring back a forgotten story.

Aunt Alice invited him to the house every Friday for dinner. He loved his time with them, hearing the stories of their childhood and of their children. There was one person whose name was never mentioned and that was Isabella. He tried hard to steer the conversation in her direction, but Aunt Alice always turned her attention to something else.

Tonight, after dinner Max would somehow bring up his mother's name and blatantly ask questions. He hoped Uncle Don had had some time to consider giving Max more of the story. He suspected there were more details than his uncle would tell.

"Hi Max, good to see you again. We're having chicken tonight, your favorite."

"Thanks, Aunt Alice. You don't know how much I appreciate this time with family every week."

Since it was just the two of them in the kitchen, Max tried something different. "Aunt Alice, may I ask you something?"

Her eyes blazed with mischief as she asked, "Sure dear. Have you met someone, and you want my opinion?"

He smiled easily and said, "No nothing like that, but when I do, you'll be the first to know. I have something personal that I hope you can help me with. I want you to tell me about my mother."

Aunt Alice pinched her lower lip with her teeth, "What do you want to know?"

"Everything. I want to know what she was like as a kid and did you and her ever get into any kind of mischief. I want to know why she got married at such a young age and most importantly, I want to know why she took me away from all of you?"

Aunt Alice took a deep breath before her knees buckled and she sank into the nearest kitchen chair. Since meeting Max, she knew this time of questions would happen and still she had not prepared herself for the moment. This young man deserved answers and as much as she wanted to share the memories with him, some were just too painful. She found it amazing how an incident in her life that had happened so long ago could come back to haunt her. It haunted her every day. Even her husband didn't know what she had done the day Max Callahan was born.

"Aunt Alice, are you alright? I'm sorry to bother you with this but I thought you could tell me about my mother before I was born. I'd like to know some about my father too, that is if you know who it is. Mom was always so tight-lipped about the whole family that it made me suspicious." He smiled and added, "But maybe I watch too much television."

Alice raised her head and spoke softly, "It's alright honey, you have a right to your family history. It's just that your mother and I didn't have the kind of childhood a person wants to remember. Your grandfather was a mean ole' cuss and your mother ran away and got married at the age of fourteen. I missed her something fierce, being she was the big sister and all. I looked up to her and at the same time I tried to protect her from our dad. She felt the leather strap more often than I did. When our mother died, he seemed to blame Isabella and made her work twice as much as a young girl her age should've. I loved

Isabella and I couldn't stand it when he hit her or made her feel worthless with his words. I helped her as much as I could. After she got married, I sneaked through the woods to visit, hoping to never get caught."

Max frowned in puzzlement, "But why did you have to sneak?"

Alice didn't dare make eye contact with Max or she knew her secret would come tumbling out of her mouth. She had never entirely shaken free of the past, but she had compressed the events of that fateful day into such a small part of her being, that opening the gate to the truth now, seemed too overwhelming. As images of that day, so long ago, ricocheted in her mind, whispers of guilt still haunted her.

"Your grandfather forbid your mother to marry Felman Young, but Felman was older and sweet talked your mother. He promised her a modern house and pretty things; something Isabella never had. He kept his word about the house and its furnishings but what he forgot to mention was what he expected from her, as his wife. Not only were the wifely duties demanded, but he treated her like an indentured slave. He was even more abusive than her father, but she was afraid of him, so she stayed."

Still not wanting to make eye contact with Max, Alice kept her focus on the dust particles floating in the bright shaft of sunlight that glittered across the floor. She wanted to break down and tell him everything, but if she did, she would have to include her husband in on the secret. Twenty-seven years was a long time to silence the truth, but now, conflicting emotions were running rapid through her mind. She so wanted to free herself of the guilt, but what if they sent her to prison, or even worse, her husband would leave her. There would be a scandal when the townspeople found out about the Sheriff and Diggor. It was so many years ago, but could they all still be held liable? How could she take that chance? It was obvious Max was not giving up his quest.

"Max, can we talk about this another time? The chicken is done, and your uncle is waiting for his dinner".

Max was disappointed but followed Alice to the dining room.

Chapter 18

SHERIFF BAXTER

Sheriff Baxter was just finishing his second cup of coffee when Diggor appeared in the doorway of his office. "We might have some trouble, boss!"

"What's wrong, Diggor, traffic light out again?'

"No sir, lights still workin, but so is Max Callahan. Did you know he has moved here permanently?"

The Sheriff stopped slurping his coffee and sat up straighter in his chair. "Where did you hear that?"

"I was over at the diner and heard Don Watkins braggin about his nephew comin' into town and gettin' hired at his first interview." Diggor limped to a chair and eased into it while establishing Max's location. "Already has an apartment and was even at church last Sunday."

"He moves fast doesn't he? Have you heard if he's been snoopin around?"

"Yea, old lady Baldwin, said he came in the library but didn't find anything." Diggor took the small flask out of his pocket and downed the liquor in one swallow. He wiped his mouth with the back of his hand and revived his speech. "That was real smart of you Baxter, all those years ago, to remove all those newspaper articles from the library. You sure was lookin ahead."

"Well, Diggor, I knew he was going to grow up and if he is anything like his mama, he's as stubborn as a mule. That day, when old Felman was shot, Isabella was in hard labor and she stuck with "it was an accident" story. I didn't believe her, but she said she knew all about the liquor ledger. She had even memorized some of the days I had been to her house to pick up my money. Yes sir Diggor, that girl was one pig-headed female. She should've been a lawyer. In between labor pains she would quote dates and numbers from that book. Said she'd turn it in to the Fed's if I charged her with murder. She convinced me to declare the shooting an accident; to say her husband was drunk and stumbled on the porch step, causing the gun to fire. The bullet went right through the jugular vein in his neck. My report had to say he died instantly."

Diggor's homely face rearranged itself into a grin, "Yea, it took a while for the old bastard to die didn't it? I think you enjoyed that."

"I don't take pleasure in seeing people die, Diggor, but I knew what kind of life that young girl had been living. He worked her like a slave and treated her like a whore. He told me many a time how he had fooled her into thinking he was going to treat her good. She was fourteen for heaven's sake. Her dad knew the kind of man Felman was, and yet he did nothing about it either. She was underage and he could've had it annulled, but I think he was glad to be rid of her. You know, one less mouth to feed?"

Among other emotions, the Sheriff was feeling a deep sense of shame. He had known the abuse Isabella was suffering at the hands of her husband, and he had done nothing about it. Felman Cooper wielded a lot of power in the Mountain Mafia.

Baxter remembered, as Sheriff, he had only to look the other way when seeing a local still in operation and it meant a lot of money in his pocket. His wife had a lot of medical needs and soon the Sheriff's unofficial paycheck was necessary. He had gotten in way over his head with the Mafia, but his wife would never have had the medicine if not for Felman Cooper. The day Felman died, Baxter felt sorry for Isabella and promised to swear it was an accident. She had kept her promise and never revealed the ledger.

"But Sheriff, why not let Max read those articles? Don't you think that would satisfy his curiosity? After all, it's the newspaper. That should be true stuff, right?" "You're probably right Diggor, but I can't go back and change things. If he keeps running into dead-ends, maybe he'll give up and just enjoy his new-found family. If his mother had told him about the ledger, don't you think he would have brought it out in the open and tried to use it against me somehow?"

Diggor lifted one brow in curiosity. "So, if he knows nothin' about the ledger, and you and me are the only ones who were there and know what happened, we're safe right?"

"That's what I'm counting on, but maybe he's just playin' it cool. That ledger could still land me in jail. There's a goldmine of information in that book. Obviously, Max doesn't know anything about it, or he would have shown it to the Fed's." I could have made the county a lot of money by issuing fines to the moonshiners, but I turned a blind eye to their business dealings."

His words held a hint of self-pity. "I was so desperate to help my wife, I just pretended I never saw a still or a bootlegger as he drove like a madman down the road. By doing that, the Mafia made sure I had enough money to buy my wife's medicine."

A silent question lingered in his eyes, but his voice remained steady as he admitted, "If I had it to do over, I probably would do it the same way. I couldn't stand to see her in so much pain. But even after she died, I got accustomed to a certain lifestyle and I couldn't convince myself to quit. I guess deep down I knew if I tried to quit, they would kill me. It was a major business during those years and finding someone stuck to a tree with a butcher knife, happened more often than anyone knew. Snitching on moonshiners or bootleggers was a death sentence for sure. Even being promised protection from the law, wasn't a guarantee."

"Yea boss, I remember. I was right there with you, don't forget."

Baxter rolled his eyes and groaned, "You were with me all right, but if anything would've gone wrong, I was the one taking the blame. Those mountain men thought of you as my little puppy dog on a leash."

Baxter leaned back in his chair and crossed his legs. "Diggor, maybe you and I ought to think about retiring. Don't ya think we've been doing this long enough?"

"Retiring? What would we do all day?"

"We'd go fishin, Diggor, we'd go fishin."

Chapter 19

MOLLY

The smell of rain lingered in the air as Molly sidestepped puddles to reach the front door of the clinic. "Good morning Jolene. Do we have a full schedule today?"

"Good morning Molly. We only have a few comin' in, but we'll have a lot of walk-ins."

"How do you know?"

"There will be a lot of accidents seeing as we had all that rain last night. The mountain gets muddy and people forget how slippery it is. We'll probably be settin' a few broken bones today."

Molly loved the sweet southern accent she heard every time Jolene opened her mouth. Folks around here had their own dialect, that long-vowel, drawn-out twang. She was also enjoying her job at the clinic. The "hill people" as townsfolk called them, brought a lot of pleasure to her days. As Dane had told her, they were a God-fearing culture, but they also lived by many misconceptions, or as they called them, superstitions. Most sounded unbelievable to her but she had learned to pretend she was interested. It seemed to form a bond between her and her patients. She did love hearing about their remedies for medical problems and had started a journal with all the treatments listed for each crisis. It was a great learning tool.

Molly was feeling more and more comfortable around the doctor which was unnerving to her. She had come here to the mountains to find peace, not to fall in love. There was nothing romantic about their relationship, but there were a few times, had Molly allowed herself, she was sure the doctor would have reciprocated. He had been quite the gentleman during the first few months of her employment and his gentleness was slowly stealing pieces of her heart.

It had been awhile since she had noticed a man, except for the guy who had rescued her from the storm. That day in the hospital she had found him disturbingly attractive. There was also something reluctantly familiar about him- she just couldn't figure out what it was. Since that day, he had invaded her thoughts more often than she would like. She had hoped to see him again, but she had quit her job before he came back to finalize the hospital contract.

Doctor Dane's nearness seemed to inflame her senses, yet thoughts of the medical supply salesman, Max Callahan, gave her heart the impression it was him she was attracted to. But why? She hardly knew him. Sliding into a relationship with the doctor would be easy, considering how she constantly found herself conscious of his masculinity. But would that be it? Just a physical relationship? The doctor had every woman in the county dreaming of capturing his attention, so she was flattered with the physical awareness she knew had ruptured between them. Even Jolene had noted the chemistry between them. With a sweet edge to her voice, Jolene said "I've seen the way ya'll look at each other. Is there something going on I don't know about?"

Molly was shocked. "What are you talking about Jolene? Have you been reading your romance novels again?"

"Yes, but that has nothing to do with it. I know hankerin when I see it."

Molly laughed, "Hankerin? What exactly is that?"

"You know, when you want to do something, but you don't do it."

"What is it you think I want to do?"

Jolene smiled a sheepish grin, "You wanna kiss him, don't you?"

Molly was too startled by Jolene's suggestion to offer any objection. She simply turned and walked into the file room. She leaned against the cabinet and thought about what Jolene had said. Did she want to kiss the doctor? Was she falling in love with him? If she were honest, she had thought about what it would be like to kiss him, but she also thought a lot about the medical supply salesman, Max. And why was she thinking of him so much? She had only seen the man twice and even though both times had been dramatic, nothing extraordinary had influenced her heart in such a neurotic way. He was even crashing her dreams. She would never see him again and the doctor was right at her fingertips. So, why not pursue a relationship with the doctor? He was super cute; kind and Molly knew he had feelings for her. Even Jolene knew. So why didn't she want to acknowledge them?

Jolene was right. Their first patient just arrived – and with a broken arm. Molly took the man into a curtained room and waited for the doctor.

When Dane pushed back the curtain, the first thing he saw was Molly, with her back to him. Her hair was pulled up with a clip, allowing loose wisps of hair to fall on her neck. He watched her for a few seconds, waiting for her to acknowledge his presence but she was concentrating so much on the patient, she was unaware of his existence.

"Good morning, Molly." He got closer to the patient and said, "What happened to you Jake? You weren't trying to roller skate, again were you?"

The ole man's beefy face brightened at the sound of the doctor's voice. "No sir, that rain last night nearly washed my Mrs. and me down the river. I was tryin' to get my dog to come in the house and I slipped on the porch steps. Darn old dog. The wind was so strong, I guess he didn't hear me."

"Well let's take a look and get you fixed up, Jake."

Molly helped Dane set Jake's arm and cast it in a matter of minutes. Jake was happy to be on his way and promised to be more careful.

"Would you like to go out for ice cream tonight, Molly?"

"That sounds wonderful. What time?"

"I'll pick you up at seven."

"Would you like to see the moonbow again?"

"It's time for a full moon already?"

"It's hard to believe but it's been more than a month."

"Sure, I'll be ready."

Dane smiled. Maybe tonight he could take their relationship to the next level.

Chapter 20

MOLLY

As the sky darkened with the first purple glaze of the evening, the moon hung low in the sky, perfect background for a moonbow. Dane and Molly followed the trail that led to the Falls, anticipating the phenomenon for the second time.

As they stood at the railing, Molly leaned toward Dane and whispered, "I don't think I will ever tire of seeing this."

Molly's seductive whisper stroked over him with the effect of a soft, warm kiss. Dane turned his head, allowing their eyes to meet; his twinkling with silent desire, hers, wide with alarm.

His voice was soft and filled with promise, "Neither will I."

Molly felt an eager affection coming from him and she had by no means been blind to his attraction for her, but until now she had never felt uncomfortable around him. Her nerves danced, her brain raced, and her stomach did a quick somersault and then it happened. He kissed her with an unexpected measure of wildness, yet soft and unhurried. His lips were more persuasive that she cared to admit but she couldn't let this happen.

Dane was her boss and she wanted to keep their relationship strictly business. She pushed him away gently and beckoned, "Please Dane, I don't think this is a good idea. You are my boss you know."

"Are you afraid we won't be able to work together if we are involved romantically?"

"I'm not sure, but if doesn't work out, it will put us in an awkward situation."

"Well then, I guess we better make sure it works out."

She smiled, thinking about it, "I'm sorry Dane, but I'm not looking for a relationship right now. I'd just like to concentrate on my career and figure out if this is where I'm supposed to be. I truly enjoy working at the clinic, and the people here have taught me so much about myself. I've been very humbled by the folks that come to see you. They have such great respect for you, as I do. I'm flattered that you find me attractive, but I can't promise you anything right now".

Disappointment settled over Dane like fog on a riverbank. He felt like he had just been gut-punched. He had waited, not wanting to rush his feelings, somehow knowing she was fragile when it came to love. But he wasn't expecting her to reject him without hesitation.

His smile had vanished, and Molly found his expression hard to read. Was he angry or had she simply crushed his ego? It was probably some of both and she felt guilty for causing such pain.

Molly spoke again, trying to sound compassionate, "I'm really sorry Dane. Is this going to affect my job?"

"No, I'm a big boy, and I've dealt with rejection before. I will admit though, I really thought you had some feelings for me." His gaze remained fixed on her face as he reasoned, "We are both professionals and we'll make it work. Who knows, someday you might change your mind."

"Thank you. Who knows, you might be right."

As much as Molly wanted companionship, she just wasn't ready. She also wasn't ready to enlighten Dane about the real reason she couldn't get involved with him. If the vision of a man in the dark, with his hands all over her, ever faded, then the chance of finding love might be possible. But until that day, having a physical relationship was a complicated subject.

She had to admit, that with her therapists help she had overcome the first step to healing, by admitting what had happened. Finding a man who could help conquer her fear and gain her trust, she felt was crucial to her over-all recovery. Someone who could understand conditions of war and grasp the meaning of combat was important to her. She had seen many Americans who had sacrificed their lives in the name of freedom. As a nurse, Molly felt every soldier's pain and suffering as they were brought into the hospital. Those who returned to base in a body bag, she mourned.

Dane drove Molly back to her apartment and as he was opening the car door, he offered her some comfort, "I hope you will take my attraction to you tonight as a compliment. I am a bit of a romanticist, but I am also a professional. I worked hard to earn my degree and I love what I do. I get the impression that you love it here too so do not let this affect our performance. We will carry on as before. Just know that if you ever need me, in any way, I'm here."

Molly gave him a friendly hug and through tears, echoed her earlier "Thank you".

Chapter 21

MAX

Max called Charlie into the living room and explained that he would be gone all day but promised to be home soon. The dog whined and rolled over on his back. Max knew this was his way of pouting. He reached down, rubbed his stomach and said, "I have to go to work if you want to eat." He opened the door on the coffee table and pulled out a bag of treats. "I'm going to put this right here so you can have some whenever you want." Max said goodbye one more time before shutting the door.

The day proved to be a busy one and Max had no time to remember the real reason he had moved to Corbin. On the way home, he noticed a billboard with an advertisement for a photography studio. The image of a man in a sailor suit flashed before Max's eyes. Silas Cooper. Who was this man? He drove a little faster, eager to retrieve the flowered box and take another look. He found it among some boxes he had yet to unpack. He carried it to the living room and turned it upside down, spreading the contents on the floor. He checked to make sure it was empty when he noticed a piece of leather hanging from an inside corner. He pulled on the lining of the box and the entire underside pulled apart, revealing a false bottom. A leather-bound book fell to the floor. He opened it quickly and was shocked to find the first recorded date was November 10, 1942. Over forty years ago. Clearly, someone had tried to hide the book. Could it have been his mother? It was with her belongings.

Max brewed a cup of coffee and sat down with the book. According to the first page, an organization called The Mountain Mafia claimed ownership. Was this the same Mafia Uncle Don had talked about? The book was divided into two sections: the production and the distribution. The production section listed only numbers, obviously some code. Under distribution, names were listed with dates and times. Max chuckled to himself as he studied this unfamiliar approach to bookkeeping. Someone with a touch of education and the gift of imagination had made the system work for over twenty years. The Mountain Mafia may not have been a legitimate organization, but they looked to succeed in their profit margins. An enormous amount of money had been exchanged in short periods of time. Names of regular suppliers were repetitive on the pages. Max found the name of Felman Cooper often, and wondered if he had been related to Silas Cooper, the sailor in the picture.

Uncle Don had confirmed to him that his maternal grandfather was a major player with the Mafia. Maybe his grandfather had found the flowered box the perfect hiding place. Had his mother been engaged in illegal action or had she stolen the ledger? The history of Max's mother was becoming more and more complicated and he was becoming more and more curious.

Max wasn't sure how much Aunt Alice and Uncle Don knew, so he was undecided as to whether he should take the book to them. If they didn't know, he didn't want to cause any more hurt for his aunt, but if they did know, some pieces of the puzzle might fit together.

He was about to close the ledger when he saw two names that looked familiar. Baxter and Diggor. The Sheriff and his Deputy. There were regular payments paid out to both county officials on the first of every month. The Sheriff was also receiving payments, weekly, by numerous code names written in the column of "accounts payable." Max was once again impressed with the unofficial encryption created by the moonshiners.

According to the ledger, Sheriff Baxter had received much money over the past years. The bookkeeper had taken a lot of time and effort to devise the codes and symbols written in the ledger, so Max studied page after page, comparing dates with codes, wondering about their meanings. He couldn't understand why someone would take such pains to hide information about the inventory, yet log in individual names. He copied a few entries, hoping to decipher the numbers. It might take a while, but it was worth a try.

He continued to the end of the book hoping to find the name Callahan or Silas Cooper. The name Felman Cooper was entered often, always beside the same number. He obviously was a major supplier. Max was confused about the Sheriffs name being recorded regularly. Wasn't he supposed to be pursuing the suppliers and the bootleggers instead of working beside them? It wasn't too hard to figure out the Sheriff was getting kickbacks for turning his head at the sight of a still or the bootlegging of moonshine. Why had no one ever questioned the lack of arrests in Boone County? Based on what he read at the library, bootleggers from Boone County had constructed the prototypes most used for making moonshine. The Fed's should have been in these woods by the numbers. Evidently, the Mafia had outsmarted the revenuers quite often, but then they did have the Sheriff on their side. He found it amazing that the local law could be so crooked and still be an elected official. Did that mean everyone turned their head to crime in this county? After all this time Baxter and Diggor were still holding their established positions. Was this ledger the only proof of their law-breaking days?

Max sure couldn't go to the local officials with his evidence, but he could go to the State Police. It was so long ago, would they even care? He didn't want his mother's name dragged out into the news and he didn't want Aunt Alice and Uncle Don to be targeted. His gut instinct told him they didn't know a lot about the ledger, but how should he approach them?

He returned the ledger to its hiding place and closed the lid. He needed a few days to plan his strategy.

Chapter 22

MAX and MOLLY

Molly rolled over and looked at the clock. 9AM! She moaned and stretched like a lazy cat before jumping out of bed. She hadn't slept that late since her college years. It felt good to be so relaxed. It was her day off and she planned to do absolutely nothing, except go to the Farmer's Market. She was fascinated with the amount of fresh produce that showed up there every weekend. She was also getting to know local farmers and their families, and she liked hearing her name called out in the crowd. It made her feel like she belonged. She always saw patients who would introduce her to other family members. Sometimes it felt like a big reunion.

As she sat at the picnic table eating her lunch, under the huge maple tree she saw a man standing in line, waiting to buy a funnel cake. He looked familiar, but she couldn't see his entire face. When he turned, she almost choked on her hotdog. It was the medical salesman, Max. What in the world was he doing here? Was he stalking her? How would he have found her? She quickly turned, hoping he hadn't seen her. She hurriedly finished her hot dog and shoved her book and half-eaten bag of chips in her tote bag. She hoped to casually walk away before he noticed her.

Standing in line for something called a funnel cake, Max saw a red headed woman sitting on a bench eating a hot dog. He couldn't be sure, but she looked a lot like Molly Carlson. He had heard she moved to Kentucky but what were the chances of this being the town. From the corner of his eye he watched her, very unladylike, stuff the remainder of a hot dog into her mouth. He followed her to the trash can and called her name. "Molly?"

Caught, nowhere to go, Molly raised her head and looked directly into big gray eyes and that gorgeous face. Pretending as if she forgot his name, she inquired, "The medical supply salesman from Willow Grove! It's Max, right?"

His response was delivered in a cool tone, "I'm flattered you remember. Yes, I'm Max. Max Callahan."

"May I be inquisitive and ask what in the world are you doing here in Corbin, Kentucky?"

Max looked down at her with unflinching directness, "Well, I guess I could ask you the same thing?"

"I'm sorry, I didn't mean to sound condescending. It's just that most people have never even heard of this place, and here both of us are standing. How did you come to be here?"

"It's a long story, but maybe I could tell you sometime if you'd like?"

He held out the flat powdered sugar treat. "I have never heard of a funnel cake before, so of course, I had to have one, but it is more than my stomach will tolerate so would you like to share this with me?" He held it out in front of her, giving her no choice but to break off a piece.

In an attempt to plop the fluffy chunk into her mouth, the sugar attached to her chin like glue. Max stared at her, burst out laughing while he quickly tried to remove the sugar with a napkin.

Molly flinched as he reached for her chin. "What are you doing?"

Still grinning, Max whispered, "Just trying to make sure you don't scare any children away. They might think you are the abominable snowman."

Molly reached for her chin and felt the sticky substance. She also could feel her irritation for Max gently vanishing as she couldn't avoid laughing.

"I'm usually a little more graceful when I eat." Pointing to the funnel cake, she asked "What is that thing?"

"You mean you've never had one either? I thought I must be the only one who had never heard of this ten thousand calorie piece of dough."

"I've heard of them, just never ate one. I was going to walk through the flea market items. Would you like to walk along?"

He was so stunned by her offer he could barely speak. The only word Molly heard was "Sure."

When Max went home that evening and thought about the day's events, he physically pinched himself to make sure it wasn't a dream. Molly Carlson, the girl he couldn't get out of his mind. The one he thought he would never see again. He had wiped sugar from her chin, and she had laughed about it. Walking through the Farmers Market with Molly had given him more joy than he had felt in a long time. She had been just as he imagined. Behind her facade of edginess and solitude, he witnessed a compassionate and fun woman. Without realizing it, she had let her guard down and revealed her true self.

"Charlie, remember the girl I told you about back in Willow Grove? I ran into her again today." He watched as Charlie yawned and went back to sleep, oblivious to his master's happiness. "Just in case you're wondering, I had a great day."

Molly had agreed to meet Max the next day and hike some nearby trails. Blue sky stretched as far as the eye could see as they rested on a plateau of rocks overlooking Corbin. A late summer breeze ruffled the leaves as they admired the silver and blue peaks of the Blue Ridge Mountains. The silence lengthened between them, making Molly uncomfortable. Max sensed the tension and even though he wasn't sure how Molly would react he instigated some innocent and lighthearted flirting. He was surprised when she implemented a few of her own attempts, ultimately melting the anxiety. It was enough for him to acquire courage to ask, "What brought you to this neck of the woods?"

Max watched as Molly's chin trembled ever so slightly and he fought down the urge to comfort her. Before she spoke, she brushed back some hair that the wind had caressed out of place. "I've always had a passion for the Appalachian people and ever since I became a nurse, I knew this was where I wanted to work. I answered an ad in the paper and found myself in the middle of these mountains. The pay's not great but the reward of meeting the people more than make up for money." She waved away a few flying insects and continued, "The people are so poor, although I don't think they know just how poor.

They are happy and most of them have great family values, even though I've heard stories about the family feuding and the moonshiners. There are so many traditions around here and the culture is so different from what I was used to. So, sometimes I'm not sure if the story I'm hearing is fact or just a good old hillbilly tale."

Max closed his hand over hers as an understanding gesture. "I've heard a few of those stories myself and some of them are pretty suspicious." Max wanted to tell Molly his story, but he wasn't sure this was the right time. She might want nothing to do with him if she discovered his family had been involved with the Mountain Mafia.

"Hello Max, I'm talking to you. Are you okay? You got something on your mind?"

"I guess I was just thinking how nice my day has turned out."

Molly smiled to herself as he spoke. He had an easy-going carelessness about him she liked. What had brought on this change? Less than a year ago, she had done everything possible to avoid him. Now she was enjoying her time with him and secretly hoped they could get to know each other better.

"I seem to have the same opinion." She glanced up at him, but he didn't give her a chance to continue. His reaction was swift, and his nearness was overwhelming. She opened her mouth to speak and his lips captured hers and for one unguarded moment, she melted into his embrace. She was shocked at her own willing response to the touch of his lips. How could she be with a man and not remember what the last one had done to her? Unwillingly, she let her mind run backwards to that dark and chilling night. The memory of the bruising kisses suddenly existed, and her body remembered the sound of the Lieutenant's voice. She pulled away, pushing at Max's chest, fighting back the tears and demanding release. The realization she was still crippled by that memory disturbed her. Max would have no way of knowing the driving force behind her actions. She wondered if she should confess her story to this man she barely knew. Impulsive action had carried her this far, but had it led to salvation or disaster? She wanted to trust his ability to listen and discern, but should she?

Max set her free from his arms as the cool air pricked his skin. He felt her shyness in the way she hesitated, in her awkward movements. An unspoken question lingered in his eyes. Had he pushed her too far, too quickly? It was only a kiss and he had felt her respond to him. He gathered his thoughts to arrange them in order, concentrating hard just to form a coherent sentence. "Molly? Did I do something to offend you?" His apologetic tone reassured her. "If I did, I'm really sorry. Talk to me Molly."

The question was a stab in the heart. How was she going to answer him? A whippoorwill called in the distance as if to say, 'tell the truth, tell the truth'. Molly lowered her voice to a confidential whisper, "I'm the one who's sorry Max." As her repressed emotions tumbled out, she sniffed and battled the tears that seeped from under her eyelids. "I know most people think when a girl is raped it's because they did something suggestive, but I was in uniform and that is definitely NOT seductive clothing. I was returning to my tent after a shift in the hospital. I was tired, my make-up had worn off and I had sweated all day.

How could that be pleasant to anyone? I'm not sure if he targeted me or if I was just in the wrong place at the wrong time." Molly sniffled again and wiped her face with the back of her hand. " I've been diagnosed with PTSD and I've been engaged in therapy for the past year. I thought I had a handle on the nightmare. One of the reasons I moved here was to plunge myself into my work. Working at the hospital was good, but my goal is to modify my environment to a simpler way of life. What better place than in the middle of Appalachian country?"

Max moved closer to Molly so he could wipe away the tears that stained her cheeks." I am so sorry you had to go through that, Molly. For whatever reason anybody comes up with, no one deserves to be put in that situation."

As though his words released her, Molly raised her eyes to find him watching her. She muttered hastily, "I hope this doesn't give you a different opinion of me since you've heard my story." She shot him a helpless female look he couldn't resist.

Max wanted to pull her into his arms and sooth her, but he would wait. She just needed to know he was here. "If anything, Molly, I see you as a strong woman, fighting for freedom from dark memories. A lot of women wouldn't be able to carry-on with their everyday life like you have done. I was in Afghanistan and I know how tough it was."

Molly interrupted, "You were in Afghanistan? When?"

"May of 2000 till February of 2001."

"Oh my gosh, maybe that's why you seem so familiar. Were you ever wounded or in the hospital for anything?"

"I was. Took a hit with some shrapnel in my right upper leg. When I got hit, I fell against a stone wall and cracked my head, so I don't remember much. The doc's removed the metal, made sure I knew my name and I was back out in the field the next week." He looked at her hopefully. "Maybe you were my nurse!"

Molly sighed, then gave a submissive shrug. "Maybe."

The two walked back down the mountain in silence but the suggestion she might have been Max's nurse captivated her thoughts enough to cause her to dwell on that time. Was it possible that he would have known her attacker? It was about time to give General Patton another phone call and ask more questions.

Max said goodnight to Molly with just a kiss on the cheek and a promise he would call her soon.

Chapter 23

MOLLY

"Hi, General Patton, it's Molly. How are you?"

"Hi kiddo, I'm great. Sorry I haven't gotten back to you but I'm having trouble getting any information that might help you. No one seems to remember anything."

"I'm sorry to hear that. I was hoping for some statistics. I have another question for you. Do you remember a guy by the name of Max Callahan while we were on tour?"

"Max Callahan. Can't say that I do. Is he dead too?"

"Oh no, he's very much alive, but he was stationed in Afghanistan same time as us. Just wondering if you knew him."

"I'll keep my nose to the ground on both subjects and call you the minute I have anything. Good to hear from you Molly."

Molly hung up feeling very disappointed. She had been so sure General Patton would come up with some evidence. If he couldn't determine the real identity of John Doe, chances are, she would never know. Maybe if she went back to the police station, she could ask more questions. What if she asked Max to go with her? They might respond better to a man.

Max had called and asked Molly if she would like to go out to dinner. When he arrived at her place, she was sitting on the front stoop waiting for him. When she stood, her pale-yellow printed sun dress revealed her gentle curves. Max was overcome with emotion when he saw her. Everything he had ever fantasized about a woman, was standing right in front of him.

"Is something wrong Max? You look upset."

"Nothing's wrong. In fact, everything is perfect. You look absolutely beautiful."

"Really? I just bought this dress and I wasn't sure about the color, you know, because of my red hair."

"It's the perfect color and the perfect dress for you."

Surprised by his flattery, Molly stood motionless, not sure what to say or do next. She watched as he opened the car door and motioned for her to get in.

Before Max turned the key, he asked, "Would you be disappointed if we didn't go to a regular sit-down restaurant tonight?"

Molly tossed him an uncertain look, "What other kind of restaurant is there, besides fast-food and I'm not a big fan."

Max crossed his arms and raised an amused eyebrow. "Have you not heard that Corbin is the birthplace of Kentucky Fried Chicken? This is where Colonel Sanders sold his first piece of chicken!"

"Are you kidding? Why hasn't anyone told me that?"

"I guess it's one of those things everyone assumes you know, so they never mention it. I thought we would grab some chicken to go, and have a picnic. I found a great spot in the park, near the water. I was hoping we could get to know each other. I'd like to know more about you and how you ended up here in Corbin."

"I'd like that too, but only if you'll share your story with me."

"It's a deal!"

The late afternoon sun cast shadows across the park as they spread their feast on an empty picnic table. Max had thought of everything: tablecloth, silverware and even a citronella candle. Molly was very impressed with his domestic skills.

"So, tell me Molly, where did you grow up and how did you end up here?"

"I grew up in the suburbs of Pigeon Forge. I'm an only child of very old-fashioned parents. My dad believed women belonged in the home raising kids and should never be allowed to do anything else. So, when I joined the Army, he was quite distraught. Wouldn't talk to me for a couple of years, but he came around when he finally admitted being a nurse is a good thing. I enlisted when I was eighteen and a year later was deployed to Afghanistan, Life was hard, but it was even harder after "the ordeal." Molly took a bite of chicken and wiped her mouth with the napkin. "I became paranoid and my personality changed. I was afraid to talk to anyone, especially men in uniforms. I thought maybe I had been too flirtatious with the soldiers so, I became completely opposite, and I didn't like myself." A bit of regret pinched her heart as she thought about that time. "I enjoyed helping my patients. I found great joy in connecting them to a loved one on the computer.

Sometimes I even wrote letters for them and when I could no longer do all those things, I fell into a depression that led to PTSD. I was so glad when my tour of duty was over, and I could come home. I was working through my issues with therapy and then you grabbed me out of the rain that dark night and transported me right back to Afghanistan."

Max remembered the eyes in the gaunt face that rainy night and he thought he should apologize for causing her so much pain, but in all reality, he hadn't meant to hurt her. He had intended for his actions to help her. "You know I didn't mean to scare you that night. I just reacted to your accident. I should have thought about how it would scare you. I feel awful knowing I provoked all those bad memories. I really am sorry."

"It wasn't your fault. Like you said, you had good intentions. As terrified as I was, it pushed me to disclose the whole story to my therapist. If that night hadn't happened, I might never have gotten to that point. I really should be thanking you."

Max wasn't sure what to say. He was happy to accept her apology, but he still felt responsible for causing her such pain. He too, sometimes struggled with nightmares that brought the war active again, so he knew the agony of remembering.

Molly, trying to gauge his reaction, broke into his thoughts, "Max, I said it's okay. Please don't feel bad."

When he spoke again, his voice was agitated, "I'm fine, Molly, but I feel as though some distant message is trying to get through to me. I don't mean to be disengaged with our conversation, but I suddenly got this de'javu feeling."

"About what?"

"About you!"

"Me? How could you have de'javu about me? I never saw you before that night in the storm."

"I don't know, but something triggered a memory. It must be from Afghanistan. We must have had some sort of contact while I was in the hospital. Are you sure I wasn't your patient while I was unconscious? I don't know where else these feelings would be coming from and I don't know why they're just now coming back to me." His voice continued to sound strained, "I feel as though some vague memory is tickling the very edge of my brain. It's like my heart suddenly remembers you."

"I'm sorry I don't remember you, but, in my defense, I did see a lot of bodies come in and out of the hospital and if you didn't stay long, I wouldn't have gotten to talk to you." Molly took a drink of water before putting forth a question, "I don't mean to change the subject but by any chance did you know a Lieutenant Walker? "

"Yes, he was my platoon leader. Heck of a nice guy. To tell the truth, we were best friends. I took a liking to him right away and then we found out we came from neighboring towns. His truck hit an IED and he got burned bad. They sent him to Germany and then I lost track of him. I tried to find him, but it seemed like he fell off the face of the earth."

"He was burned?"

"Yea, pretty bad. He wasn't one to talk much about his family, so I had nothing to go on. He had a girlfriend, but she was Hispanic, and his parents said if he married her, they would disown him. I guess they too were from the old school."

Molly couldn't believe what she was hearing. What if Lieutenant Walker was John Doe? The same man that raped her. Max's friend. She would call General Patton with this information and hopefully find the truth. Would Max believe her when she told him his friend had assaulted her? How and when would she tell him?

Molly steered the conversation away from war stories and launched into telling her childhood antics involving the neighborhood kids. It was fun to relive those carefree times and share them with Max.

"It's your turn Max. I can't wait to hear about some of your mischief."

"I don't think we have time for that tonight. It's getting dark and we need to clean up our leftovers and our trash. My story can wait for another time. Besides, it gives you another reason to see me again."

Molly smiled in contentment, "I'm not sure I really need a reason."

Chapter 24

MOLLY

As soon as Molly walked in the door, she called General Patton. "I'm sorry sir, for calling so late but I have some information I think will help find John Doe."

"Okay, slow down girl. What do you have that's got you so excited?"

"You're not going to believe this, but I've met this guy who was friends with Lieutenant Walker whose truck hit an IED and he was burned really bad. Max lost track of him after he was sent to Germany."

"What makes you think it's him?"

"Let's just say I have a strong hunch. I met him in Afghanistan. Remember I told you about finding that silver charm called a Hamsa? His girlfriend had given it to him, and he never took it off. Maybe it was her footprints in the cemetery. But how would she have known he was there?"

" Do you know her name and where she's from?"

"No, I only know she's Hispanic"

"Okay, well I'll see what I can find out. Hang in there. We'll figure this out."

"Thanks, General. Talk to you soon."

Molly had trouble sleeping that night; thinking about Max and Lieutenant Walker. How was it possible Max could have had such a good friend and not know about his nighttime activity? Maybe he did know! If he knew, he had done nothing about it. What kind of man lets his friend get away with rape? Should she be worried about Max? So far, he had been the perfect gentleman. But so had Lieutenant Walker during daytime hours. How was she going to approach Max about this issue?

The next morning, Molly dragged herself out of bed and got ready for work. She arrived a few minutes early and grabbed a cup of coffee. Dr. Dane came out of his office to say good morning and to give her the schedule. "You look a little tired today, Molly. Didn't sleep last night?"

"As a matter of fact, I didn't, but I'm ready for someone to cheer me up today."

"Well then you're going to like our first visit. I'm going to take you to Chrissy Taylor's today. She has ten children and it's a pleasure to call on them. Most well-behaved kids you'll ever know."

"Why are we going to see her?"

Dane smiled, "Cause she's pregnant with number eleven and she can't get to the office with that many young'uns. He licked his lips with his tongue and said," When she knows I'm coming she makes me the best blueberry cobbler this side of Atlanta. I usually get a whiff of it as I'm climbing the mountain. Hope today's no different." He picked up his bag and started toward the door. "You're gonna like her, I promise."

Molly followed him to the car, trying to keep her mind on what Dane was saying, but thoughts of Lieutenant Walker kept creeping into her head. Was he really John Doe? Was he really dead? She wanted to tell Max, but how? If she told him she had found his friend, she also had to tell him that Lieutenant Walker had raped her. Would he even believe her?

"Molly, are you listening to me? Did you bring that bag of candy I laid on the counter?"

"I'm sorry, Dane, I'll run back in and get it."

"I can't go to the Taylor's without candy. The poor youngin's would never taste the stuff if I didn't treat them when I go see their mother. I buy candy in bulk, but even if I only gave them one piece, they would still be so appreciative."

Molly looked at the doc and smiled. He had a heart of gold. One she was sure she could love. So, why was she always thinking of Max?

As they pulled into the grass in front of the small house, children came from everywhere. Some came out from behind bushes while others tumbled out the front door. They were all talking, but two words were consistent – Dr. Dane! They were quiet as they crowded around her and the doc, as if waiting for something. Pretty soon, Dane pulled out a bag and their little ritual began. He loved teasing them and they loved pretending they were sad. Soon there was candy flying in all directions and Dane was laughing so hard he was crying. The fun soon was over, and each child took his booty and ran in different directions. Dane completed his exam of Chrissy and made her promise to find him if she needed any help.

Chrissy patted the Doc on the back and said, "After doing this ten times, I think I know what to expect, but I promise."

Molly gave Chrissy a friendly hug and returned to the car. Dane followed and as he turned on the ignition, he turned to Molly and spoke softly. " You seem to be far away today, Molly. Are you by any chance homesick?"

"Homesick? Homesick for what?"

"Maybe for your family?"

"I'm not very close to my family."

"Would you like to talk about it? I'm a pretty good listener."

"Nothing to talk about, really. When I joined the Army, my dad was upset and didn't speak to me for years. He thought I should have married a hometown boy, had kids and stayed at home, just like my mother did. But he showed no more respect toward my mother than if she would've stood on the street corner. He holds a lot of disdain for women. My mother was basically a slave for him." Defiance glittered in the dark depths of Molly's eyes. "I made up my mind a long time ago that I would not fall into that category. My dad thought he owned my mother and she was afraid to cross him. He would always refer to the passage in the Bible about how women should submit to their husbands, but he never read any further. You know, about husbands love your wives? I suppose in his own way, he did love my mother, but he had a weird way of showing it. It left a lasting impression on me."

"I'm sorry your homelife had such a negative impact on you. I hope you don't think all men are like that. "

Molly's anger abated somewhat under the warm glow of his smile. "No, I've been around enough men to know that most of them treat women with respect, even if they don't like them. My dad was brought up by parents who lived through the depression and they were hard core. You did things their way or you didn't do them at all. He's cut from the same cloth, so to speak." She felt embarrassed for spewing her family's adversities to Dane. "I'm sorry, you didn't ask for a homily of my homelife. I try not to think about it, but when I do, I guess my emotions take over and I start rambling."

"No need to apologize. I told you I'm a good listener."

She had not wanted Dane to see her vulnerability, but too late for that. Would he change his opinion about her? What would it matter? He was only her boss and even though he had tossed romantic hints her way, her heart hadn't responded. But she did have to work with him every day and so far, the working atmosphere was great. She didn't want to jeopardize that.

"Thank you for your kindness Dane. I shouldn't have laid all of that out in the open for you to hear." "I'm glad you did Molly. It gives me a better insight into why you seem so sad. You're a very capable nurse and you have a competent way of handling yourself, yet I've noticed the mask of privacy you wear. I also sense you have something else in your past that you're running from. Is that why you came here, to Appalachian country? Did you think these mountains would hide you from the injustice you've suffered in your life?"

"How do you know I've endured injustice?"

"It's in your eyes, Molly. Even though you smile a lot, there's a sadness in your face, and your mannerisms speak louder than words."

Molly's head bobbed in agreement. Time and painful memories had eroded away her confidence. She knew it was time to start a new chapter. "I guess I know that. I just don't want to admit it and I don't know how to resolve it."

"If there's anything I can do to help, Molly, all you have to do is ask."

"Thanks Dane."

Chapter 25

MAX

Max dropped by the Farmer's Market to pick up a fresh cherry pie, on his way to Aunt Alice and Uncle Don's house for dinner. Of course, he couldn't walk by the whoopie pie counter without purchasing a dozen. He peeled back the plastic wrap on one and ate the entire piece of cream filled chocolate before he returned to his car.

Coming every Friday night to dinner had given Max opportunity to get to know his extended family better. He had gotten used to his uncle's dry sense of humor and his aunt's response to him. They made him laugh with their innuendoes to each other, but it was obvious they were still in love after all these years. Conversations about Isabella had not been part of Friday nights for the past few months and Max was getting antsy about being kept in the dark. He decided tonight he would bring up his mother's name and no matter the reaction he would ask questions. He wanted to know about the ledger book. Why was it in his mother's possession? Was she part of the Mountain Mafia and that's why she had to skip town, or was she a victim of her husband and father? Had they made her leave town, taking the book with her?

Every question he had, led back to why had his mother taken him away from the family? Soon after her husband died, she had left the mountain. Had someone pressured her into leaving? Why would she threaten to kill herself if family members tried to contact her? Had she committed a crime, and if so, why hadn't she been arrested? He was sure the Sheriff or Diggor would know, but something told him not to approach them just yet. Besides, it was a long time ago, so why was everyone so afraid to talk about it? Surely no one could still be prosecuted. And prosecuted for what? He didn't even know if a crime had been committed. That was tonight's goal - find answers.

'Hi Max, come on in. Dinner's almost ready." Aunt Alice pointed to the big pot on the stove. "We're having pot roast tonight. That was one of Isabella's favorite meals."

Max was shocked. Alice brought up his mother's name. Maybe tonight could be productive after all. He saw the empathetic look on Alice's face when she spoke her sister's name and he hoped she might be feeling a bit melancholy about Isabella. As soon as dinner was over, he must get Alice alone and with any luck, she would bare her soul to him about his mother.

The pot roast with all its trimmings was wonderful, but Max was so anxious about his after-dinner plans, he barely ate anything, blaming his loss of appetite to the whoopie pie.

While Uncle Don and Bruce sat in front of the television catching up on Friday night football, Max made his way to the kitchen, picked up the towel and dried dishes.

"You don't have to help with this Max. Go on in and sit with the men."

"I don't really follow football, and besides, I want to spend some time with you, Aunt Alice."

"That's nice dear. It has been a while since we've chatted."

Good. At least she was open to conversation, so Max verbalized his thoughts. "Aunt Alice, I don't want to keep bringing this up, but I'd really like some more information concerning my mother. I feel as though she did me a real injustice by keeping me away from all of you. I used to hear other kids talk about family reunions and holidays with their families and I would wonder what that would be like." He came close, looking down at her intensely, "Believe me, I regret not having that in the past, but I am so grateful to you to be given the chance to enjoy it now. Being able to spend time here with my family is a dream come true. The best part is, you've all treated me as though I've always been here. I truly feel like I belong. I never had that feeling before."

Alice gave Max a look of compassion but also of worry. "I've been doing a lot of thinking, Max and you're right, you do deserve to know what happened and I think I'm ready to tell you. But when I do, I don't want to ever talk about it again, so your Uncle Don needs to be with us when the story is told. He thinks he knows what happened, but he really doesn't." She crossed the kitchen to the back door and stepped out onto the deck. She sat on the glider and motioned for Max to sit beside her. She called for Don to join them during half-time, but while waiting for him to stroll outside to a chair, Alice unveiled some mountain history to Max.

"Have you heard of the Mountain Mafia, Max?"

"Max wasn't sure if he should mention the ledger now, or wait, but Alice seemed eager to talk so he said, 'Yes, I have."

"I'm not sure how much you know, but years back if that name was mentioned, people changed the subject or literally walked away from the conversation. Unless you were one of them, you didn't talk about them. They were the elite residents of the mountain, or at least that's what they had everyone believing. People were afraid to cross them and anyone in their right mind would never betray them."

Alice became silent for a few minutes, as if she needed time to say her next thought. "In the defense of the Mafia, they did have a good side to them. A lot of people received help from them. Financially, I mean. But, of course, if they helped you, you were forever in their debt. Fathers, whose families were near to starving would help bootleg the moonshine, in all kinds of weather. Sometimes even the wife and kids had to help and in exchange, they would receive food to last them till spring. If you were in that position, trust me, it was expensive food, but for some, they were left with no choice." Alice stood and walked to the railing, taking her time with the history lesson. "It wasn't only residents of the mountain that the Mafia helped financially. Some elected officials also found themselves beholden to the Mafia."

Max interrupted. "Are you talking about the Sheriff? Sheriff Baxter?"

"I am. Baxter was quite young back then and he had a sickly wife. She needed expensive medicine and without the Mafia's help she would have died way sooner than she did. Even after her death, Baxter continued to look the other way when the revenuers came to Boone County. According to him we had some right smart moonshiners in these mountains. Always seemed to slip by him without a trace."

Alice peeked in the door to check on the football game and see how long she had before halftime. "Baxter got paid good money for his blindness. There was a code between him and the Mafia that pissed off the revenuers. They even tried to infiltrate his strategy with the moonshiners, but they always left the mountain empty-handed. The mountain men came up with a plan for portable stills. Everything was on wheels, ready to be moved at a moment's notice. To this day, Federal Agents have never figured out how the moonshiners were always one step ahead of them. Those city boys in their shiny shoes, spent many a night under the stars, listening to coyotes, waiting for a bear to eat them alive and yet they camped, hoping to catch a bootlegger with gallons of white lightning. The folks at the general store loved putting ideas into those city slicker's heads about all the wild animals and how hungry they were." Alice gave a deep hearty chuckle. "They carried shotguns the size of Daniel Boone's. The good-ole boys that didn't need the Mafia sure got a kick out of telling stories to the Fed's."

Alice paused to allow her heart to stop its frantic hammering. Should she continue with all this information or just say enough for tonight? But she felt compelled to continue. She would not allow a moment of doubt to steal away her peace of mind; something she had been waiting for since the day Max was born.

"I have to tell you that your Grandfather was a high ranking official in the Mafia. He was a mean old coot, and no-one crossed him. Especially his family. I told you before how I tried to protect your mother because he seemed to get his jollies by beating her or degrading her till she wilted like a flower with no sun. He found it very amusing. At fourteen, your mom was physically mature but emotionally she did a lot of dreaming, of course. Felman Cooper came along and made a deal with the devil – your grandfather. Felman offered to take her off his hands and he basically said, good riddance. Felman was a very superficial man but Isabella couldn't see that. She saw nothing but promises of a good life with pretty things to decorate her home. She had never had the privilege of having something to call her own, so she grabbed on to his words and married him." Alice shook her head disapprovingly. " Little did she know, but her life with him would be far worse than with her father. Now, she was not only his housekeeper, but he destroyed her ability to ever be with a man. He overpowered her with sex and used her as a whore. She lost herself in her own world. It was the only way she could survive. She shut everyone out except me. Her eyes constantly had a blank stare, but I always imagined I could see the real Isabella dancing and smiling like we used to do in the woods, far from the house."

Max was mesmerized with the story. No wonder his mother never wanted to talk about it. He couldn't believe he was part of such dishonorable ancestry. "So, Aunt Alice, what is the secret about all of this? And the ledger. Why did my mother have it?"

Alice came off her seat. "Your mother had the ledger? How do you know that?"

"Because I have it now. I found it among her personal items."

Alice whispered, "Have you told anybody about this? Does the Sheriff know?"

"No, you're the first person. Why? What would it matter after all these years?"

"I'm not sure, but that ledger is a piece of history. The government searched this county high and low for that book. It had information in it that could have put Boone County on the map. Years ago, the FBI even came snooping around, determined to find the famous ledger but found nothing. I'm not even sure they knew how it existed. Have you had a chance to read it?"

"Yes, I have, and I was shocked at some of the names in there. Now granted, most of them were unknown to me but a few like Sheriff Baxter, Diggor, Felman Cooper and of course John Callahan, who I'm assuming was my grandfather."

"Big bad John! That was him."

"If my mother was married to Felman, why didn't she go by the name of Cooper instead of her maiden name?"

"For the four years of her marriage, she was known as Isabella Cooper, but the instant old Felman was pronounced dead, she took back her maiden name. She had her reasons. I promise I'll tell you because it is important."

Max needed a drink of water. His throat was parched, and his head was swirling in all directions. How much more could there be to this story. He felt like he was in the middle of a movie and he couldn't wait to hear the ending. He retrieved the bottle of water and returned to the deck. Uncle Don and Bruce followed him, indicating they were in a rush to get back to the game.

Alice motioned for the two to sit down and be patient. "What I have to say is going to affect all of us and I don't want you to rush me."

"For heaven's sake, Alice, get on with it. This is an important game."

"Then you better go set the recorder, cause I don't think you're going to be watching it tonight."

Don lifted both hands in mock surrender, then sat down and crossed both arms over his chest. Bruce followed his dad's behavior.

Alice bowed her head and silently said a short prayer. The three men looked at each other, not sure what to expect. Did she know something about a world disaster or what?

"Let me begin with, Don, you know I love you dearly and I would do anything for you. I also have never lied to you, but I have kept something from you all these years. Please let me finish the story before you say anything."

Don nodded his head, indicating he would obey her wishes.

"Going back in time to when Isabella and I were kids, even though it was a long time ago, is still very fresh in my memory. You've heard the stories of our childhood, Isabella's being worse than mine. When she got married, that left me alone with our father. He was different with me than he had been with Isabella. He wanted her to be with him all the time, but me, he didn't care. I could be gone all day, and he didn't even seem to notice. So, I spent as much time as I could at Isabella's, but it had to be when Felman wasn't home. He didn't want her to have any contact with anyone, especially her family." Alice looked directly at Max and said, "The bigger she got with you, Max, the more help she needed around the house, and of course, her husband did nothing for her except hit her or push her. She was already past her due time, when I came by one day to check on her and bring some fresh tomatoes, but Felman was home and I heard him yelling at her. I hid behind trees until I got close enough to see inside the house. I saw him push her into a table and she started to bleed. He laughed and told her to get up."

Alice ripped out the next words impatiently. "I was so angry that I started throwing tomatoes at him, but he laughed again and told me to go home. I didn't even think about what I was going to do. I just did it. His rifle was leaning against the door frame on the back stoop, so I picked it up, aimed, and shot the man dead. I remember asking him, "Who's laughing now?" Isabella went into shock over what I did but she was in so much labor pain, she couldn't concentrate on Felman. We heard yelling outside, and Isabella grabbed the gun out of my hands and just held onto it. She told me to hide."

Alice pressed both hands over her eyes as if they burned with weariness and her body wilted with relief. She waited for a response from those listening, but the silence was deafening.

Don finally spoke. A slight tremor of anger tainted his voice. "You killed someone, and you never told me? I thought there were no secrets between us?"

Tears that had threatened to fall moments ago now ran down Alice's pale cheeks. A jolt of panic ran through her. What would happen to her and Don? Would he walk out? His wife was a killer. How did she expect him to react? "I'm sorry Don. I was just a kid when it happened, and I worked hard at locking it away in a dark place. Seeing Max brought everything to life again, and I knew I had to tell you. I know I should have told you even before we were married but I was so in love with you and I thought you might walk away from me if you knew the truth. I've carried this around for so long, I'm glad you finally know. Every time I hear a knock on the door, I wonder if it's the authorities coming to take me to jail."

Don rose from his chair and pushed in beside Alice. He put his arm around her shoulder and said, "You mean to tell me that for the last twenty-seven years you've lived with this fear? How did I not pick up on that? I'll admit I'm a little upset, only because you didn't trust me enough to talk to me." He cupped her chin in his hands and said, "Alice, you were just a kid. How did you get away with such an act? The story, as it was told in the general store, was Isabella shot him in self-defense. Even then, I remember the gossip. Isabella had a lover and she shot old Felman so she could be with the sailor."

Max almost fell off the glider. The sailor, the one in the picture, the one that wrote, Love, Silas? He really was his father? "Wait a minute. Felman Cooper is not my father?" He looked at Uncle Don. " How do you know this?"

"I don't know that for sure, Max, but you sure do look like Silas."

Max fought the urge to laugh out loud. All the stares he had from people in town could be explained now. They must have thought Silas Cooper had found an age-defying cream that made him look young again.

'Is Silas still alive? Whatever happened to him and why didn't he and my mother marry after Felman's death? Is Silas Felman's son?"

Alice held her hand up motioning Max to stop. "Too many questions too fast Max. The question I can answer for sure is yes, Silas is Felman's son. I do know for a fact that yes, your mother was seeing Silas whenever she could, which wasn't that often. He wanted to tell his old man he was in love with Isabella, but she was afraid he would kill him."

Max was shocked, "Kill his own son? And my mother was married to such a monster?" I can see why she thought about shooting him!"

Alice added quickly, "But she didn't shoot him, I did."

Don was sitting quietly, taking in all the conversations, watching his wife relive a horrible moment in her past, observing his nephew trying to grasp this information about his mother and wondering what could happen next.

Don picked up Alice's hand and covered it with his. "I'm sorry, honey that you thought you had to carry this burden all by yourself, but I think we all want to know why no one was charged?" He looked at Max and Bruce. "Let's give Alice a chance to finish her story."

Alice let her mind wander back in time as she saw Isabella bleeding and helpless, lying on the floor. Felman dodged a few tomatoes and was yelling at Isabella to get his lunch. The whole time he was laughing; sounded just like the devil. He had his foot raised, ready to kick her when I picked up the rifle. I'd never even shot a gun before. To this day I don't know how I had the strength to pull the trigger. I do remember landing on my butt from the kick of the gun." Her features softened as she thought about Isabella and her eyes burned with unshed tears. "She was my big sister and I adored her. I swore that I needed to protect her but she always sheltered me. Sheriff Baxter and Diggor had been on their way for a meeting with Felman when they heard the shot. They were in the house within minutes. When they saw the gun in Isabella's hand, they immediately assumed she had shot Felman, but she was deep into labor and they weren't sure what to do. Isabella asked them to fetch the midwife, so as Diggor ran out the door, he passed the Sheriff. I saw Baxter put his finger to his lips, indicating for Diggor not to tell a soul about this. I can still hear Diggor say, 'No sir, boss, quiet as a mouse.' As soon as Diggor left, the Sheriff wanted answers. Isabella told him she had gone into labor and Felman had attacked her, so she shot him in self-defense. He wasn't buyin it, he said. Felman was too smart for that. He also knew who buttered his bread, so to speak, but when Felman moaned and the death gurgle got louder, Baxter stood over him and I swear I saw him smiling." Alice's voice, fragile and shaking, but determined, continued her shocking confession. "I was hiding in the bedroom for what seemed like hours, so Baxter thought Diggor, himself and Isabella were the only people who really knew what happened. But it was just me and Isabella who knew the truth. I could hear Baxter telling Isabella that as soon as she had this baby, she would be charged with murder. But my cool sister looked him right in the eyes, between labor pains, and said 'I don't think you want to do that unless you're going to be keeping me company', which of course made Baxter laugh. He said, 'Now young lady why would I want to do that?' This time she laughed and said, 'Because I have the ledger and I've memorized the lines with your name on it."

"Baxter turned white as a ghost. His face lost all expression and left it stone cold. I think he almost threw up, but he gritted his teeth and fought down the anger that was choking him. I watched as Isabella struggled to keep her composure in between labor pains. Baxter stood over her, straining to hold his temper. I really thought he was going to hurt her, but she raised her chin and refused to cringe under his anger. I guess he had never had anyone threaten his authority before, especially a woman."

"Next thing I knew, Isabella was spittin out these names and dates and even amounts of money, right down to the penny. Baxter was in shock. For the first time ever, he was speechless. Finally, he yelled at her to stop. I remember Isabella's exact words that day. "You say Felman tripped on the porch with the gun, it went off and he died, or I'll bring out the ledger and give it to the Fed's. I'm sure I'd be a real hero for exposing you and Diggor. You two won't see the side of this mountain for a long time. Or, the mafia might get to you before the Fed's. I know you've seen men stuck to trees with a knife and left there to die. You do not want to be one of them. What do you say Sheriff?"

Alice took a drink of iced tea and kept talking. "He grabbed the gun from Isabella just as Diggor came bursting through the front door with a midwife. She cried and Baxter told her to shut up and do her job. Isabella was screaming in pain and I was trying to stay quiet. Diggor asked what happened and I guess for the sake of the midwife, which was known for her incessant gossip, Baxter declared Felman dead from a self-inflicted gunshot wound. I remember seeing Isabella smiling and with one last push, Max, you came into the world screaming too. I couldn't wait for the funeral truck to come get Felman and take him out of our lives for good. When it was only Isabella, you and the midwife, I came into the house pretending I had just walked in."

"Wow, that's some story Aunt Alice. How have you kept that a secret all these years?"

"I had too, for your mother."

"But if you kept a secret so she wouldn't go to jail, why would she cut you out of her life like she did?"

On safer ground now, Alice reflected a moment. "I'm not sure I can explain the bond Isabella and I had as sisters, but she took the blame for my actions and she wanted it to stay that way. She was afraid if she stayed here, someone would figure it out. This way, by her leaving, she thought people would forget about it and since I was so young, she also didn't think anyone would suspect me. That's why she took back her maiden name. When she moved away from the mountain she didn't want to be associated with the name of Cooper. Felman was well known in these parts and even in other counties. She didn't want anyone to know that she had been married to him."

Sobs finally crumbled Alice's composure as she tried to speak. "I don't want anyone to think of me as a murderer.

To this day, I really think he would have killed Isabella, and you too, Max if I hadn't pulled that trigger."

Don was the first to speak, followed by Max and Bruce. "Trust me Alice, none of us could even begin to think that way. I think we can all agree. It took a lot of courage to do what you did, so don't think about the life you took, but the two lives you saved. But what is this ledger you talk about? Obviously, it was quite important and how did Isabella have possession of it?"

"That I'm not quite sure of. Isabella could be a bit wily at times, so I suppose she found it and studied it. I'm so glad she did. It sure came in handy."

"So, what ever happened to the ledger? Was it ever found?"

Max thought this would be the right time to reveal his discovery. "I have the ledger at my place."

Uncle Don looked shocked. "You have the ledger? How did you get it?"

"It was among my mother's personal items; hidden I might add. I only found it by accident. Now that I've heard the story, she must have gotten to it before the Mafia officials. I'm surprised she got away with it."

"She almost didn't. The Mafia came looking for it one day, but they never found it. They waited a few months and when no charges were filed against anyone listed in the ledger, they quit their pursuit. Nothing was ever been mentioned about the ledger again."

"So, it's not that important, is it? The only thing that might cause a disturbance is the fact that Sheriff Baxter and Diggor are listed on its pages. Could they still be held accountable?"

Max heard the uncertainty in Uncle Don's voice. "Can't really say I have an answer to that Max, but since those two are the law around here, I bet they would make sure the information never got to the state level. I always knew there was something crooked going on in the Sheriff's office, but they always won the elections. Now I know why. When you're in law enforcement and you turn a blind eye to the Mafia, your future's well secured. I remember a group of locals, once, who tried to oust the sheriff by claiming he was taking kickbacks but every one of them ended up involved in an accident or financial hardship. Too bad that ledger wasn't brought out in the open back then."

"My mother kept her end of the bargain but I had nothing to do with that so I could take it to the Fed's if I wanted too, right?"

"How much do you really want to be involved with this Max? You're new here, you don't know the ways of the locals."

"Alice spoke up quickly. "What if they found out the truth about Felman? I don't want to go to jail!"

"Aunt Alice, you're not going to jail. It was ruled an accident and that's what it was."

Tears clouded Max's vision as he tried to reassure Alice that without her fearlessness, he wouldn't exist. "I am so grateful to you Aunt Alice. I owe my life to you. You're my hero!" He leaned over and gave her a kiss on the cheek, tasting her salty tears. "I think we've heard enough for tonight. You can finish the story later when you're feeling up to it."

"Thank you, Max. I'm so glad you came home."

Chapter 26

MAX

Max coaxed Charlie out the front seat of the car and walked with him into his apartment. The dog found a comfortable spot near his toy box and went to sleep. Max collapsed onto the couch and laid his head back. He thought it had been a lot to comprehend when he discovered he had relatives, but Aunt Alice's story was even harder to wrap his head around. What was he supposed to do now? Pretend none of this ever happened? He still had the ledger with the criminal proof against the Sheriff and Diggor. But what should he do with it? Take it to the State Police? It was a long time ago and would it even hold up in court? Most of the Mountain Mafia were deceased or out of business. Besides, who would benefit from the ledger being made public. It was the only proof that moonshining had existed and had been very profitable. But who would care, in today's world?

Max was happy Aunt Alice had finally rid herself of her burdensome secret, but he still didn't know why his mother had the ledger or why she hadn't married Silas Cooper. And the thing he wanted to know the most; was Silas his biological father and if he was, was he still alive?

Sleep came nudging in among Max's thoughts that night. He lay awake imagining what it would be like to meet his father. What if Silas Cooper wouldn't acknowledge him? Even his mother had never disclosed his father's name. Who exactly, he wondered, did she register on his birth certificate?

Max bounced out of bed, wide awake and made his way to the closet. He took down the flowered box from the shelf and dumped its contents on the floor again. He tore the fabric from the inside where he had found the ledger, looking for the document but nothing else was in there. Disappointed, he continued to sort through the remaining papers. If he couldn't find his birth certificate, he would send to the state for a duplicate. He needed to know. When the time was right, he would press Aunt Alice for more information.

He took the picture of Silas Cooper, the young sailor, and clipped it to the refrigerator door. If he stared at it enough times, maybe he would see the resemblance.

Chapter 27

MAX

Molly was enjoying her Saturday afternoon at the Farmers Market staring at the homemade pies and cakes, debating with herself if she should buy one, when she heard two ladies talking about Max. To get a little closer, she pretended to be picking out some ripe apples. The lady with the blonde hair piled high in a god-ugly outdated do, seemed to have the most to say. "Did you hear Max Callahan came back here to live?"

Her friend had inch long fire-engine-red fingernails and was almost as wide as she was tall. "Yes, I had heard that, but I still haven't seen him anywhere in town. "I've heard he buys a lot of whoopie pies here on the weekends. How are we going to know if it's him?"

"Because if the rumors are true, that he's a clone of Silas, then we'll know him for sure. The rumor back then was his mother was having an affair with Silas while she was married to Felman, his father."

"I used to know Silas, before he went to the war. He used to hang around at the café, but he disappeared after his father died. I remember the rumors and they were awful. Everywhere you went, people were talking about it.

Supposedly, Felman, Silas's dad, fell on the porch and shot himself but everyone said Isabella, Max's mother, shot him. Everyone also said he deserved it, cause he was so mean to her." She picked up an apple and rolled it around in her hand as if weighing it. "You know, she gave birth to Max the same day her husband died."

The lady with the fingernails looked like she was going to cry. "Isabella had a rough start in life and it wasn't fair what people were saying about her. We used to sit together in church. I always felt sorry for her, being so poor and all."

"But they really weren't poor. Old man Cooper just wouldn't spend any of his money, especially on Isabella. Maybe another rumor, but he was supposed to have said his wife would be alive if it hadn't been for Isabella's birth. What kind of man says that?"

"A mean ole cus, I guess. Are you buying any apples or not?"

Molly couldn't believe her ears. If what they said was true, no wonder Isabella gathered up her son and left, not only the county, but the state as well. No one has skin that thick. She called Max on the phone and asked if they could meet for dinner tonight. She was glad he agreed. She really wanted to hear his story.

Max had never told her much about his mother or why she had kept him away from family but after hearing Miss Up Do and Miss Fingernails, she was curious now. She hoped he would trust her enough to tell her all he knew.

At dinner that night, Molly decided to be brave and just come right out and ask Max about what she had heard in town. "Max, you promised to tell me about your childhood and why your mother took you away from here. Do you feel like talking about it now?"

"Sure, but I still don't have all the facts. I just don't feel like I can push my Aunt Alice real hard. She's finally been able to talk about what happened, but I know there's more and I'm going to have to wait till she feels like talking again."

"I understand, but I don't know anything. I need to be honest with you. I heard two ladies talking today, in town, about you and I felt as if they were talking about a celebrity. They're waiting to catch a glimpse of you to see if you look like someone named Silas. Do you know all about this?" Molly sighed as she asked one more question and waited. "Who is Silas?"

Max waited, while the waitress poured more water into their glasses. When she walked away, he gave a loose-muscled shrug. "The rumor is, he is my biological father, but I have no proof. I guess I look a lot like him, that's why people stare at me in town. They're in shock that Silas is back in town and doesn't look a day older than when he left twenty-seven years ago."

Molly's thoughtful expression turned into a worrisome frown. "Don't you want to know if that's true?"

"Well of course, I want to know, but no-one seems to know the truth. I think Aunt Alice knows, but she's so fragile at this point, I'm hesitant about bringing it up again."

Endless questions bombarded Molly's thoughts, but now wasn't the time. She would wait until he was ready to tell her.

Max took a few bites of food and voluntarily told Molly everything he knew about his ancestors. When he was finished, Molly felt tears running down her cheeks.

Chapter 28

JOHN DOE

Molly went to work Monday morning thinking about John Doe, or was his real name Lieutenant Walker? How was she ever going to find out if the man in the grave was her attacker? How was she going to approach the subject with Max? When he had talked about Walker, she could tell he had quite the admiration for his friend.

Jolene was calling for her as she walked out of one of the exam rooms. "Molly, could you come here for a minute? I need some information."

"Yes, Joleen, what is it?"

The young girl flashed Molly her angelic smile while shoving a form in front of her. The county wants your driver's license number, since you have an out of state plate." She then added with eagerness, "Unless you're going to apply for a Kentucky license. But, meanwhile, could you please fill that out, just so I have it on file, if those rascals come snoopin around." She winked and handed a pen to Molly.

Molly retrieved her purse from her desk drawer, ready to copy numbers but her license was nowhere to be found. She removed everything from her wallet and searched piece by piece. No license, but her rummaging caused a small photograph to fall to the floor. Not recognizing it, nor having time to ponder over it, she threw it back into her purse. She had patients waiting and they were more important. She promised Jolene her license when she found them and escaped into an exam room before Jolene could protest.

Molly had just set the leftovers on the counter when the doorbell rang. She was surprised to see Max standing outside her door. She invited him in and offered to share her meatloaf sandwich and coleslaw. He accepted and found it to be tasty. "How about we top this off with a shared banana split? I hear the Dairy Dell makes a mean one."

"That sounds wonderful and I'll take you up on that offer, but only after I find my driver's license. If I don't have that tomorrow when I go to work, Jolene's liable to fire me. She needs it to be on file."

"Okay, I'll help you look. Where might it be?"

"I've already looked in my purse and my wallet but I'm going to dump both on the floor and really look good this time. I was in a hurry at work."

Molly turned over the purse and Max watched as everything, but the kitchen sink fell out. "I've never seen all the contents of a woman's purse before. This is quite interesting. How do you know what to carry in here? Is there a general list that women follow or is each one different?"

Molly laughed at him. "You're really not that innocent, are you? Didn't you ever see inside your mom's purse?"

"No, she was a very private person and when she claimed ownership to something, you didn't question it."

Max was gently examining each object from the purse when he picked up the small photograph to study it a little closer. When he did, he stared, complete surprise on his face. How in the world did this picture get in Molly's purse? He had seen this before. It was Lieutenant Walker's grandmother. He was sure of it.

Molly saw Max's expression change when he looked at the photograph. "Do you know that woman? It was in my wallet this morning when I was searching for my license, but I don't recognize her. But I do remember where I got it. I found it on the floor in the hospital tent in Afghanistan. It must have fallen out of a soldier's pocket, but when I asked around, no one seemed to recognize it, so I stuck it in my pocket. I just don't remember keeping it."

"Well, I can't be sure, but it looks like the same photo of my platoon leaders' grandmother. He kept it in his shirt pocket, over his heart."

Fear, like the quick, hot touch of the devil shot through Molly as she remembered the night of the attack. She would argue that Lieutenant Walker did not possess a heart.

"Molly, are you okay? You look like you've seen a ghost!"

"I just may have heard you talking about one."

"Walker's grandmother? She's no ghost. As far as I know, she's alive and kicking. According to her grandson, she's quite the feisty old lady. He had some real funny stories about her." Max's smile relaxed and his disposition abruptly changed. Nodding, implying that he was convinced of his thoughts, he said, "Walker must have been one of your patients."

Molly deliberated on what path to choose: play the victim, which in this case she was, or forgive Lieutenant Walker and never tell Max what happened. But why couldn't she do both? If she and Max were going to have a relationship, she needed to be honest with him and keep no secrets. But telling him might affect their harmony with each other. Since Max's bond with Lieutenant Walker was strong, he might not believe her account of the attack.

Molly struggled to keep the anger she felt from her voice. "He might have been. You have to understand, when there was an assault and multiple men were brought in, we didn't have time to learn their name, or sometimes, depending on where they were hit, we never saw their face. Burn victims were usually shipped out as soon as possible to discourage infection."

Something about Molly's behavior struck Max as being uncharacteristic. Her mannerisms implied she was experiencing a great deal of anxiety. Something he had noticed every time they talked about the war. "We don't have to talk about this, Molly. It seems to make you uncomfortable."

Molly's voice was quiet yet held an undertone of cold contempt. "I'm sorry for my behavior, but you're right. I do feel angry and humiliated when I remember my time in Afghanistan. I told you a little bit of what happened to me over there. The only other person, besides you who knows about it is my therapist. I want to tell you the whole story but it involves someone you know and not only am I embarrassed, but I'm afraid you won't believe me."

"Why wouldn't I believe you? I've found you to be most credible in everything we've ever talked about."

His teasing grin tugged at her heartstrings and she exhaled an exasperated sigh, trying to sweep away her tangled emotions. She was conscious of the dull throb of regret she seemed to carry around all the time. Regret she walked alone to work that night. Regret that no one heard her scream. Regret that Lieutenant Walker felt the need to overpower her. Regret she couldn't let the memory of that night disappear.

Max sat, right foot on left knee, waiting for Molly to respond. Another trait he had learned from his mother – patience. He did not attempt to cover the fact that he was watching her. He could see her trying to hold back tears. He reached for her hand with gentle authority and said, "Molly, I'm a very understanding man. What is it that you can't tell me?"

The minute his warm hand touched her arm, she felt safe. His nearness comforted her and she was glad he was with her. There was no reason she couldn't answer his simple request.

Tears fell as Molly told her story. Max listened, like he had never listened before. He shoved the ugly image to the back of his mind, but not until the dismal thought burned his heart. He sat quietly, comprehending the words Molly had just spoken and reflecting on the many hours he had spent with Walker. A lot of their conversations had been about women, but nothing had triggered any warning signs to Max. Maybe there were two Lieutenant Walkers, but deep down, he knew that wasn't true.

Molly was waiting for an answer and Max felt obligated to concentrate on the present, instead of Walker, whom he knew was dead. He carelessly realized Molly was not aware of Walker's death.

"Molly, I'm not exactly sure what to say, except that I do believe you. Sometimes people have dark sides, that they don't show to everyone. I only knew Walker for about six months, but in that time, we did become good friends. It's very disturbing to think about what he did to you. If he were still alive, I would turn him into the authorities, but not before I forced him to admit what he did and why."

Molly jerked her head around to stare at him. "Lieutenant Walker is dead? How do you know? Are you sure?"

"He pulled rank on a few of the clerks and got me listed as next of kin. If something happened to him, he wanted me to be the first to know, so that I would be the one delivering the news to his family. After the explosion, he was sent to Germany and he found ways to make my visits happen." Max blinked furiously to hold back the tears. "It was awful, seeing him like that. He was wrapped up like a mummy and could barely speak. He made me promise to send word to his family that he had died. He had already started the ball rolling with paperwork. I fought him on that decision, but in the end, I succumbed to his wishes. Through one of those same clerks, I found out that he was still alive and had returned to my hometown, looking for me. My tour had been extended and I didn't make it home as scheduled. By the time I set foot on American soil, he had already died. I heard the plea to identify John Doe on the radio so I went to the morgue, but pretended not to know him. His family had already suffered so much. Even though they didn't have a body, they had come to terms with his death. I couldn't open that wound again."

Molly noticed the tremor in his hands as he talked about Walker.

When I came back home, I read in the papers how they had buried John Doe in the County Cemetery. I went to visit him and tell him how sorry I was and that I wish I could tell his family where to find him."

"It was you?

"It was me, what?"

"It was your footprints! I was riding my snowmobile when I saw the fresh tracks in the cemetery, and I followed them to the grave. I also found a Hamsa laying by the cheap headstone. Did you put it there?"

"I did. Walker never took it off. Said it was his good luck charm. He truly believed it would protect him from evil. One of the Afghanistan interpreters in our unit introduced him to the significance of the Arabic Hamsa symbol, convincing him if he wore it, he would be safe from all evils. Walker wasn't a religious man, but I think he felt as if God would save him, just for wearing the Hamsa. He was a proud man, in many ways, and wearing that necklace allowed him to show that he did believe. Whether it was a belief in our God or just a Middle Eastern symbol, he never said. When I cleaned out his locker, I found it. I guess I'll never know why he wasn't wearing it the day of the explosion."

Molly remained uncomfortably still. What could she possibly say? The hunt for John Doe was over. The man who had raped her was dead. Should she feel different now, knowing the two were the same? Did she still feel so adamant about finding his family?

"I'm going to take you home Molly. I think we both have some thinking to do

Chapter 29

MOLLY

The first thing Molly did when she returned home was call General Patton. He would give her his opinion and then she would have to decide what she could live with. The burden of not forgiving, on her shoulders for the rest of her life, or forget the name of Lieutenant Walker forever. As beneficial as that sounded, she doubted the reality.

"General Patton? How are you. This is Molly."

"It's so good to hear from you. I hope you have better news than I do."

" I do. Lieutenant Walker is dead, and he is definitely the John Doe I've been looking for."

"Why is that good news and how do you know for sure?"

"To make a long story short, my friend, Max, was in Lieutenant Walker's unit, knew he had been burned badly and had been sent to Germany. He then returned to Willow Grove, looking for Max. He pulled strings to have his family notified of his death, before it happened. Max read the newspapers about John Doe, went to the morgue to identify him, but didn't, because of the promise he had made to Walker, concerning his family. Lieutenant Walker didn't want any of his family to see him after the explosion. He wanted them to believe he was dead."

Molly took a deep breath and continued, "There's more. Lieutenant Walker raped me while we were in Afghanistan and threatened me if I ever told."

"He what? Molly why didn't you ever tell me?"

"For the reason I just said. He threatened my position in the Army and my nursing career. How ironic is that I wanted to help John Doe, who turns out to be my attacker? Then I meet a guy who was his best friend. I wanted to see the guy put behind bars, but he had a worse fate. He got caught in an IED explosion and now he's dead. I don't know how to feel." Molly sniffed and held back her tears.

General Patton couldn't believe what he was hearing. Molly had been raped! How long had she been enduring this burden by herself? He thought carefully about his next sentence. "Molly, I'm so sorry that happened to you. It's a little late now, but is there anything I can do for you?"

"Just being my friend is a big help. Thank you for always taking my calls and for all the work you did to help find John Doe. It's so disturbing to think that all I wanted for him was to find his family, so they could have some closure, and he turns out to be the man who raped me."

"You did that because that's the kind of person you are. Not many people would take the time to help find a dead man's family. Don't let this incident change who you are Molly. What he did to you is not unforgiveable. I understand how you think it should be but don't let one evening influence your heart for the rest of your life. You're a strong woman and you're a survivor. Don't let one man's lust and stupidity dictate the way you live. You can use your situation as a support system for other women who have been in your shoes, so to speak."

General Patton imagined he could hear Molly's tears falling as he waited for her reaction to what he had just said.

When Molly finally spoke, she sounded severely defeated. "Thank you so much for saying all those things and I promise I will think about that. Thanks for all your help and for being such a great friend and mentor. Please keep in touch."

"I'll call you soon and see how you're doing. Take care."

Chapter 30

MAX and MOLLY

Molly pulled herself together and called Max. Life was too short to allow friendships to fall apart. She would make the first move and discover his reaction. She did have to wonder what Max meant when he said they both have thinking to do. Was he having second thoughts about their relationship? Did he think of her now as "spoiled goods"? Conversation on the ride home from their last date had been unpleasantly strained and Molly's skin had prickled at the tension radiating from Max.

When they had arrived at her apartment, she opened the car door, said goodnight and bounded up the steps to her front door. Inside she had collapsed to the floor in tears. Seemed like that's all she was doing these days.

Max had driven out of Molly's driveway wondering why she was upset with him. Her unexpected declaration had caught him by surprise. His mind was still reeling with the information Molly had told him. Not that he didn't believe her, it was just so out of character for Walker to have done something so heinous. Max needed time to process the details. So, he wasn't the best communicator, especially with women, but he could remember nothing he said to Molly that would have offended her. Her reaction to discovering Lieutenant Walker was dead, surfaced as a real shock. Max wasn't sure if she was happy he was dead, or if she wanted him alive so he could be prosecuted.

It had now been four days since she had talked to Max and they had passed slow. After hours of soul searching, and assessing her life, she determined that General Patton was right. She didn't want to play the victim. That would get her nowhere but depressed. She had done nothing wrong the night Lieutenant Walker attacked her and she was done feeling guilty. She was sorry he had died and she felt empathy for his family, but she should move on, and put it in her past. Maybe God was using her as a tool to help other women in similar situations. Like her, there would be women, right here in Corbin, carrying this burden secretly. Starting a support group for women of all ages sounded like a great idea.

Max had just sat down at the dinner table when his phone rang. "Hello, this is Max."

"Hi Max. It's Molly. Are you okay?"

"Yes, I'm fine. I've been thinking about you."

"You have? Why didn't you call me?"

"Embarrassment mostly. I just can't get over the way I acted toward you and

I've been trying to figure out what to say. I'm so sorry about Walker. I feel somewhat responsible. I have to be honest with you. I knew he had done something to a woman, but he would never tell me who and what. I guess deep down I didn't want to know, so I never pressured him into telling me, and that was really cowardice of me. When you told me the story, I was so ashamed of myself. I couldn't have stopped what he did, but I could have reported it, so you might have had some justice. Who knows, he might even still be alive."

"Are you willing to get together tonight? Maybe we can talk this thing through so both of us can continue living without guilt or shame."

"I'll pick you up at six. We'll stop at the market for dinner. Things never seem as bad when I'm wolfing down a whoopie pie."

Molly smiled and laughed out loud.

Chapter 31

SILAS

Max thought more and more about the ledger and less and less about who could be put in jail because of its contents. He had this feeling that the Sheriff knew more about Felman and Silas Cooper than he admitted. Maybe he would hand over that information if Max surrendered the ledger.

Being so involved with his relatives gave him a new perspective on the true meaning of family. Not only could he count on Friday nights with Uncle Don and Aunt Alice but so often additional kin showed up. He was still learning all their names. But he still felt a void about his father. If old Felman was his father, then he would close the case, as he did not want to acknowledge him as a father, but if his son, Silas proved to be his biological father, then he wanted to find him and get to know him. He needed to know the reason Silas never married his mother.

Before he picked up Molly for dinner, he stopped by Uncle Don's. He needed some advice.

Max knocked on the frame of the open screen door and watched as Uncle Don hurried to open the door. "This is a nice surprise." He gave him a fatherly hug and added, "I hate to tell you this, but we're only having leftover's tonight for supper."

Max, laughed and said, "It's okay, I'm not here for supper. I have a date with Molly. I just came for some advice."

"Ask away. What's on your mind?"

"I want to know if you think I should take the ledger to Sheriff Baxter and make a deal?"

"And what kind of deal would that be?"

"I want to know if there's any proof that Silas Cooper is my father and if he's still alive?"

Uncle Don's brow creased in concentration. "What makes you think the Sheriff knows the answer to those questions?"

"I'm not sure he does, but I thought the ledger would give me some leverage and he could find out for me. I really need to know. If Silas is alive, I want to meet him. I want to know why he left my mother."

"So, you came here for my advice, right? Well, my advice is stay away from the Sheriff. He hasn't been a trustworthy official in this county for the past forty years and I doubt that he's going to change. In the past, he was elected because of the Mountain Mafia. In recent years, I'm not sure how he's managed it. People in this county don't take kindly to change, so as the old saying goes, "if it ain't broke, don't fix it. He's such a familiar and strong force in this community, no one ever runs against him at election time."

Max scrubbed his hand across his face in frustration. "So, what should I do now? I just can't let it go."

"Get on the computer. See if you can find a Silas Cooper. I think it's time all the rumors were put to rest and you discover your real heritage. There's DNA testing now so you can be sure. It was wrong of your mother to keep such secrets from you. If there's anything we can do to help, just let us know."

"Thanks Uncle Don. I agree with you. It's time I knew."

Molly was excited when Max told her his plan and before they went to dinner, they typed Silas's name into the computer. More than one Silas Cooper was found but knowing his approximate age, they narrowed it down to one. His place of residency was listed as Denver, Colorado. Max copied the phone number, folded the paper in half and stuck it in his pocket.

Molly asked, ""Don't you want to call him now?"

"I do, but I can't think on an empty stomach, so let's get some dinner"

Max and Molly ate little. Max was concerned how he would start a conversation with a man he was accusing of being his father. Would Silas even want to talk to him? He didn't want to bombard him with questions but if he was his father, Max hoped there would be a chance to salvage the relationship.

Back at Molly's, Max picked up the phone and dialed the number. It rang three times before a male voice answered. "Hello, Coopers."

"Hi! Is this Silas Cooper?"

"Yes, who is this?"

"My name is Max Callahan. My mother was Isabella Callahan."

The man said her name softly, "Isabella. Is she still alive?"

Max felt his knees go weak. It was possible he was talking to his father. After all this time. "No sir, she passed away about four years ago." There was silence on the other end of the line and Max waited, not sure what to say next.

"How old are you son and when is your birthday? "

"I'm twenty-eight and I was born on September 4, 1962."

"That's the same day my father was killed and I was told it was an accident but I never quite believed that. My old man was too skillful a hunter to be involved in a mishap like that. There was a rumor that reached me, even when I was out to sea, that it was your mother who shot him."

"Yes sir, I have heard that, but I have been reunited with my mother's family and the truth has come out. There was a lot going on during that time. I've also been told that you are my father. If that's true, I was hoping to meet you."

Silence thundered in Max's ears. And then the roar of the dial tone.

Max was confused. Did Silas hang up because he was in shock, which meant he didn't know he had a son or did he just want nothing to do with him? He wasn't sure what to do now except wait. He couldn't force the man to accept him into his life.

Chapter 32

MAX

Silas found his way to the nearest chair and sank into it. Isabella had a son. His son. Why had she never told him? They had planned on having many children when he returned from the war. They also had a plan that Isabella would divorce his father, Felman and move far away from the mountain.

He would never forget the first time he met Isabella. She was already married to his dad but he had fallen in love with her at first sight. They had tried their best to keep their love confidential but the mountains had a way of detecting secrets.

Silas was in a submarine in the Pacific Ocean, on a secret mission, when he received word his father had died. There was no way he could get home for the funeral and had no way of communicating with Isabella. Knowing a divorce between his father and Isabella would no longer be necessary, comforted him. Isabella could now continue living on the mountain and not be in fear of the Mafia.

He wrote letters expressing his love and his eagerness for Isabella to become his wife. He wrote almost every day in anticipation of receiving return mail from Isabella. But nothing ever reached his mailbox. After six months, he quit writing. He was heartsick and embarrassed. He made a vow to never return to the mountain and never to mention her name again. He had kept that promise until this day.

It saddened him that Isabella was dead but he was ecstatic over the fact that she had a son and he was alive. And he was trying to find his father. His father. Silas Cooper. Dad. He always wondered what it would feel like to hear someone call him Dad. He never understood why Isabella had discarded him like an old sock, and he had been too proud to go back to the mountain and find her reason. Many a day he came close to returning, but pride had kept him away. Why hadn't she told him about his son? Why had he allowed his arrogant pride to prevent him from returning to the mountain and finding Isabella? He never allowed himself to fall in love again, realizing now just how much he had missed.

Silas sat down and returned the call to Max. When the young man answered, Silas spoke with excitement, "Hi Max, this is your father speaking. I can't wait to meet you."

Silas found his luggage and walked through the airport doors to the outside waiting area. The mountains seemed to stare at him at him, calling his name. The overcast sky held the promise of rain but nothing could conceal the blue summits of the mountains he used to call home. But with his return came so many memories. Harsh memories with his father, but wonderful memories of Isabella. With his eyes closed, he remembered each moment they had spent together. He consoled himself with the reminder he would not waste time trying to change the past, but he was here to embrace the future.

He watched as a young man and woman parked their car, got out and held up a sign with the name of Silas written in big bold letters. Without warning, tears flowed down Silas's cheeks as he waved to the young couple.

The reunion was awkward at first but it soon became obvious that they were destined to be reunited. Soon, conversation flowed and Silas recounted local stories of long ago. The three went straight to Max's apartment, giving Silas some time to recover from jet lag.

The next morning, Max asked Silas if he would start at the beginning and tell him about he and his mother's romance and why they never married. Max wasn't prepared for what he was about to hear.

Silas towered over Molly's small frame as they stood by the kitchen counter waiting for the coffee pot to quit perking. He asked for the sugar and poured at least two teaspoons into the dark liquid. His appreciative sigh told Molly it suited his taste. He walked to the couch and stretched his long legs out onto the ottoman, waiting for her and Max to sit.

"The first time I saw your mother, I was in total awe. Our ill-fated love began that very moment. I remember her blue eyes. They were so expressive. Sometimes she didn't even have to talk. She would just look at me and I knew exactly what she was thinking. We had such a connection. It was like a spiritual connection." A faint smile touched the corner of Silas' mouth. It was a few seconds before he continued. "I couldn't believe she was married to my old man. She was too young and too innocent. I used to cringe every time I saw how he treated her. I know I shouldn't say this, but when I got word that my dad was dead, I shouted hallelujah. The first thing I thought about was Isabella's freedom. I started counting the days till I returned to the mountain. I wrote letters to her, every day. We were out in the middle of the Pacific, so mail wasn't all that regular, but nonetheless, I wrote every day. A month passed, then two. Before I knew it, six months had gone by and not a word from Isabella. I decided I was nobody's fool and I quit writing. When I got discharged from the Navy, I thought about going back and seeing her but I was too mule-headed. I couldn't understand why she hadn't written. I would have blamed it on my father, but he was dead, so that theory held no water. To this day, I don't know what happened. In all these years I've met no one as beautiful as your mother. I still have her picture on my bedside."

Max refilled Silas's coffee cup in silence and returned to his chair.

"I'm so glad you reached out to me, Max. I realize you physically look like me, but you are so much like I remember your mother. I so wish I could have been there all those years to help her, especially when she got sick."

Max shifted in his chair and looked directly at Silas. "There are some things that went on around here, with your father and my mother that I think you should know. It involves the Sheriff too. Before you left for the Navy, I'm sure you knew your father was involved with the Mountain Mafia, right?"

"Yes, I followed him in secret to many of his meetings. Meetings that involved moonshine and ways to outsmart the Feds. I could have testified to a lot of secrets, but Felman would threaten to kill me if I ever breathed a word of their plans. I was young and I had seen what my father could do to a man and his family. When folks disappeared, it wasn't because they moved out of the county."

Max and Molly both were shocked at his confession. How could these men have such power over other humans? No wonder Silas never came back home.

"I have something to show you, Silas, I guess I mean Dad. It's a box my mother had for many years and I never saw the contents until after her death. I found a picture of you in uniform and a few letters from her folks. There were no letters from you. If she kept your picture, don't you think she would have kept your letters? I've been thinking about that and I'm wondering if she ever got them. But why would anyone not allow a young woman to receive letters from a soldier during war?"

Max was silenced by the dark, angry expression that had settled on Silas' face.

In two simple words, Silas answered. "Felman Cooper."

"But Alice had already shot him. He was dead. How could he have gotten to the letters before Isabella?"

Silas took a sip of coffee, savoring the dark mellow flavor. He remained silent, but the look in his eyes was as turbulent as a violent storm. Molly and Max regarded his angry stare as an acumen to what he was certain had happened to the letters. They waited with muted curiosity until he was ready to talk. When he did, they listened and whole-heartedly agreed with his plan.

The next evening Silas, Max and Molly stood outside the residence of retired Postmaster Henry Hoover. They rang the doorbell and when the old gentleman finally opened the door, he recognized Silas immediately. "Come on in Silas. I've been waiting for this visit for a long time." He simply stared at Max and smiled.

"Then I guess my hunch is right. You know why we're here!"

"I do. I'm just sorry it took you this long to figure it out. It's hard for me to look you in the eye with all the shame I feel. I regret doing what I did, but at the time, I didn't feel I had a choice. I'm old now and no matter what the Sheriff does to me, once he finds out I've told the truth, doesn't really matter anymore. My wife passed a few year ago and I'm a lonely old man." With a moan of distress, Henry broke down in tears.

Silas wasn't sure what to do. He had never seen a man of his age cry before and he didn't know how to comfort him. And did he really want to? This man had been part of the conspiracy to keep he and Isabella apart. Even under the threatening circumstances from the Sheriff, Henry should have tried to do the right thing. Interfering with the mail is a felony, even in those days.

Silas reached for the tissues on the table and handed the box to Henry. "Obviously you regret the part you played in all of this, but could you please tell me exactly what happened?"

Conflicting thoughts stirred Molly's emotions. She knew the old man had done wrong but no one sitting here had walked in his shoes and they shouldn't be so quick to judge. She quickly moved beside Henry and picked up his hand in hers. "It's okay Henry, we're not here to punish you. We just want the truth, all of it. Everything you know."

Henry pulled himself together, blew his nose and confessed to his days of being a coward. "Sheriff Baxter had control of this town back then." He sniffled and continued. "Of course, he still does, but now we do have a few folks who stand up to him. He's not quite as confident as he used to be. The Mountain Mafia no longer operate in this mountain and when they moved on, they left the Sheriff behind to fend for himself. He looks over his shoulder a lot. When he found out Max had come back to town, he was a nervous wreck. He and Diggor both."

Max was listening intently but he had a question. "Why did the Sheriff care if my dad and mother wrote letters back and forth?"

"Your grandfather, Felman, knew they had been seeing each other behind his back and he was furious. He was very cunning, Silas. Did you know he hunted you like an animal? He used to watch you and Isabella in the woods. He didn't love your mother but he didn't want anyone else to love her either. Typical case of pure jealously. Even when it involved his own flesh and blood."

Pieces of memory fitted together for Silas. He remembered the eerie feelings he and Isabella both felt when they met in the woods. After all these years he now discovers that the someone was his own father. What would make a father hate his own son to that degree?

Henry felt sorry for Silas, as he watched his face collapse into a horrified expression. He wasn't sure there were any words he could say to comfort him, so he resumed his story. "Felman and the Sheriff used to meet behind the post office and exchange their obligations, as they called them. They didn't know about the old mail slot in the rear of the building. They used to stand right on the other side of it and plan their actions. They had no idea that I could hear them. There were some things I could prevent from happening, if it involved the mail, but Felman himself, paid me many visits, backed up by Sheriff Baxter. I knew better than to cross either one. I was relieved when Felman was killed, but within hours, the Sheriff came into remind me of the covenant I had made with Felman. That's what he called it, a covenant. Made me feel like I had made a promise to God, but deep down I knew it was the devil. And yet, I maintained my fidelity. Felman had threatened me and my family for years. Said if I didn't go along with his plan, I would wake up one morning as a fatherless widower. The Sheriff reminded me of that every week." He blew his nose again and tried to smile. "Silas, I know it's too late but I know for a fact that Baxter kept every one of those letters. Yours and Isabella's. I don't know if that was Felman's request, or if Baxter was jealous and just kept them for spite. I don't blame you if you take this to the Feds. Messing with mail is a federal offense and you could get a warrant to search Baxter's house. Between that offense and being blind to moonshiners all those years, the Sheriff could spend his last years in jail. Although, I could too, given what I've done." He broke down in tears again, mumbling his regrets.

    Silas got up reluctantly, hating himself for causing such distress to an old man. Henry had lived in fear most of his life and he deserved some freedom. After an affectionate slap on Henry's shoulder, Silas held out his hand, offering a truce. The gesture contained an understanding that Henry had not expected. His tears continued to fall, now resulting from pure gratitude.

Chapter 33

SHERIFF BAXTER

Diggor came rushing through the door of the sheriff's office, out of breath.

"Who you runnin from?" Sheriff Baxter burst out laughing. Your wife chasin' you again?"

"I don't think you're gonna be laughing when you see who's comin in the parking lot."

"Who is it? Silas Cooper? I'm not afraid of him or his son." In an all too familiar stance of arrogant authority, Baxter stood by the window, waiting to see the mysterious visitor. When he saw the blue blazer and the shiny badge attached to the young man's belt, he had the sickening sensation that his life was about to plunge downward.

The door opened and the Federal Agent stepped inside. He stood as if he prided himself on his good looks. He also looked like a man determined to find the pearl in the oyster. "Sheriff Baxter?"

"Yes sir, that's me. What can I help you with today?"

"I have a warrant to search your house so may I suggest you find your house key and come with me."

"Search my house? What for? What could I possibly have that would be of any interest to you?"

"When we find it, then you'll know. Let's go."

Baxter was surprised. He couldn't imagine what he had that the Fed's were interested in. Maybe they thought he had the ledger. If that was it, they were in for surprise. They could tear his house to pieces and they sure wouldn't find that piece of evidence. If only he knew where it was. A slow, evil smile spread over his face as they pushed him into the back seat of the Cadillac.

The Agent took Baxter's house key and opened the front door. Within minutes four other agents filed into the living room. Each was given orders where to search. The Senior Agent handcuffed Baxter to a kitchen chair and searched kitchen cupboards.

Baxter was not fond of housework and the agent was not being kind about returning items to their original locations.

"Look, if you tell me what you're looking for, I'll tell you where you can find it so you don't have to tear up my house. That is, if I have it."

"Okay, hot shot, we're looking for some letters."

"Letters? Letter's from who?"

The agent's mouth flattened into a hard line. "If you're going to play hardball then just tell us where you keep old mail. Do you have an attic? Or maybe we'll have to tear your office apart too."

No more pretending. Now Baxter knew what they were talking about. Felman had bought a fireproof safe for Baxter to make sure no one ever found the letters. He still couldn't figure out why Fed's would want some old love letters. There was nothing attached to them that would prove he had anything do to with moonshining. He laughed again. He had nothing to worry about. Max didn't have the ledger, or he would have turned it in and they wouldn't be looking for such silly evidence.

Baxter couldn't quit smiling. He was positive they would not find the ledger in his possession. They must be pretending they want the letters, but it's really the ledger they're looking for. As much as he wished the ledger was in his possession, these ole boys were barking up the wrong tree. Wait till he sued them for wrongful accusations.

"Hey Pretty Boy, I just remembered something."

"Oh yea, what it is? Suddenly know where some letters are located, do you?"

"There's a big black safe down in the basement in the far-right corner. The letters were put in there for safe keeping. The combination is written on the first page inside the Bible. Couldn't get much safer huh?"

By this time the agent was feeling his anger building. He drilled his index finger into Baxter's chest and asked the location of the Bible.

"On the bookshelf."

Within minutes the letters were recovered and the Sheriff, still handcuffed was once again shoved into the car. "Hey you can't keep me in handcuffs. I cooperated with your search. You have nothing on me."

"We'll see what the judge and jury have to say about that."

"Judge and jury? What are you talking about? I've been Sheriff for the past forty years. I need to know what the charges are. No one in this county will go against me."

"I wouldn't be so sure about that. Witnesses are lining up to testify as we speak."

Baxter's skin crawled as he looked into Pretty Boy's face, expressing plainly that as far as he was concerned, the Feds could all go to hell, especially this one.

Chapter 34

SHERIFF BAXTER

The Sheriff's trial was scheduled for the first Tuesday in October. That meant he would have to sit in isolation for two weeks. The local news station was planning to broadcast it so even if people couldn't attend the trial, they could sit in front of their television sets.

Sheriff Baxter sat in the jail cell and shook with powerless rage and fear. No one would tell him what he was being charged with. He was allowed no visitors, not even Diggor.

By the end of the first week, Baxter was so furious he could hardly speak but when he did, his voice was loud and belligerent. His body seemed to vibrate with anger. The county sent lawyers to talk with him, hearing his side of the story. They couldn't plan a defense without knowing the charges. All the Fed's would tell them was, it concerned mail fraud and a ledger.

The most recent lawyer to visit was Attorney Bigler. He was a no-nonsense guy that stood tall as an old oak and his body was just as sturdy. His Rolex looked out of place on his massive wrist. His imported espadrilles with jute soles allowed him to glide to the offender's cell with little to no warning. In past assignments he had discovered his sudden appearance always gave him the upper hand on the one behind the bars.

"How you doin today Sheriff?"

Baxter's eyebrows jerked up in surprise. "Well maybe you should tell me. I'm stuck in here like a rat in a trap. I have a right to know what's going on."

"Yes, you do. But then so do I. Why don't you tell me about the letters and the ledger?"

"I've already told the Fed's about the letters and I don't know anything about the ledger."

The edge of the attorney's mouth twisted into a knowing grin. "So, someone entered your name, quite a few times I might add, in a book that you know nothing about? I think that would be dishonest, don't you? Do you think we should round them up and ask them why they did that?"

Baxter could feel impatience firing a spark of temper in Bigler's eyes. He resembled a predator ready to pounce. He gestured with his hands for Baxter to sit down on his bed. When he did that, the ring was immediately noticeable. The vibrant diamonds forming the letter M shone bright in the center of pure gold. The Mountain Mafia mark of power. Evidently Bigler was part of the Mafia.

Baxter hadn't seen a ring like that in years. He knew he was doomed if any of Bigler's family had been listed in the ledger. He himself, had never seen the famous book, so he had no idea whose names were listed, except his own and Felman Cooper's. If Max Callahan had not come to town snooping, he would be resting his feet on his desk this very minute instead of standing in front of a member of the Mafia who had been sent here to defend him. How ironic to be defended by his adversary. His chances of being vindicated just became slim to none.

Bigler's shoulder leaned against the door frame of the cell and glared at the Sheriff. "Not going to talk to me today, huh? That's okay. I may have been instructed to defend you but I'm not going to try very hard. You've been a crooked official your entire four terms and it's time you pay for your actions. See you in court." He stepped out into the dank hallway and locked the door.

For the first time since his wife had died, the sheriff broke down and wept. His shoulders slumped in despair and a deep agonizing grief threatened to overcome his will to live. He had nothing left in this world. He didn't even have his job. He was under the impression the entire town was feeling hostile thoughts toward him and the only person he considered family was Diggor. He wasn't even sure where his friend stood during all of this.

He sincerely felt remorseful for his past behavior, even though he had been blackmailed. He was supposed to be the law in Boone County and instead he had allowed himself to be tolerant of inexcusable crimes. Bitter regret tugged at his conscious as he continued weeping. He remembered how proud he had been when he won the election to serve as County Sheriff. He had believed it to be an honor to take an oath to uphold the law. Sitting here now, he couldn't quite remember the exact year when his integrity had taken a turn toward corruption. Had he only been more resilient to temptation, his life might have been different. Need of money, in his younger days, had influenced his unwise decisions when the reprehensible Mountain Mafia men had approached him.

Not a church going man, he never understood the power of prayer that people talked about. He had no right to ask God for any favors at this stage in his life, but maybe he should try. If God loved everybody like that street-corner preacher used to yell, then maybe he should ask for forgiveness. Forced to be alone for the past week had allowed him time to reflect on the past forty years. Without a doubt, he knew he deserved to be found guilty.

Chapter 35

The Trial

For four days the court room was full. Max and Molly attended every day, along with Don and Alice. It was heartbreaking for Max's relatives as they heard Alice testify about the day Max was born. The State of Kentucky had filed documents stating Alice's acquittal so she was free to finally tell the world the truth.

Diggor also testified about that day, and how Isabella had forced Sheriff Baxter into claiming Felman's death as an accident. It had been a real shock to everyone, including Diggor and the Sheriff, that Isabella had not been the shooter. The judge recognized self-defense as Alice's motive and the fact that she had been only ten years old, allowed her exoneration.

Sheriff Baxter's part in mail fraud was confirmed by the testimony of the retired Postmaster. He stated how fear had kept him from reporting the issue to the mail commissioner all those years ago. As the memory came back to haunt him, his composure on the witness stand was overcome with shame and remorse, causing him to break down in tears.

As the witnesses testified, one by one, Sheriff Baxter was in awe of how many people had been influenced by his actions during the years. Not all the testimonies were accusations; people also spoke in defense of him and he was grateful for their words of encouragement.

On the fourth day, when court was called back into session, it was because the jury had reached a verdict. Baxter could barely breathe. Weary, he leaned forward on the table and cupped his head with his hands. He wasn't ready to hear the word guilty.

"Foreman of the jury, do you have the verdict results for Mr. Baxter?"

"I do, Your Honor. On the first count we the jury find the defendant guilty of mail fraud. On the second count, we the jury find the defendant guilty of concealing illegal moonshine stills and bootlegging practices, resulting in many accidents and deaths. We would like for you, as judge, to take into account the circumstances that manipulated the Sheriff into those situations. Even though we have found him to be guilty of crimes that happened a long time ago, we feel he should be punished. We have some suggestions if we could meet with you in your chambers later today. Thank you, Your Honor."

The spectators were relieved by the verdict, yet surprised at the jury's request. This would be on the local news tonight for sure.

Inside the judge's chambers, the jury members made it quite clear even though they wanted to see punishment for the sheriff, they all agreed that spending time behind bars would only cost the county more money and accomplish nothing. Baxter would be permanently let go from his position, and a temporary sheriff would be appointed till next election. He would receive none of his pension, having to sign over the entire amount to the county for reimbursement of penalties and fines never collected from moonshiners and members of the Mountain Mafia. Community service would also be on the list as part of his punishment. The judge listened carefully to each suggestion and then smiled. "I would like to commend each and every one of you for your response to this case and for your perceptive insight. I find it to be very shrewd, but prudent. I am going to set in to motion all that you have suggested. Thank you for you service in my courtroom. You are all to be commended." The judge dismissed the jury and returned to his bench, ready to disclose Baxter's sentence.

When the judge repeated his penance, exactly as the jury had suggested, Baxter fell to his knees. He had never felt so appreciative as when the handcuffs were removed and he was released into the custody of Deputy Diggor.

Chapter 36

FAMILY

Max invited Molly to dinner at Alice and Don's and, like Max, she fell in love with the entire family. When they arrived, they found Silas sitting in the living room chatting with Don, while Alice prepared dinner. After introductions, Molly stuck close to Alice in the kitchen, hoping to acquire some cooking knowledge.

Max was surprised, but pleased to spend some quality time with his dad. For the past twenty-eight years, his life had been like a puzzle with one piece missing. Now with that one piece found, his life could fit together and be complete.

After dinner, the conversation drifted to the past week's events at the courthouse. "How do you feel about the Sheriff's sentence?" asked Uncle Don. Do you feel it justifies what happened to your mother and the secret your Aunt Alice had to carry around with her for all these years?"

Everyone could hear the doubt in Max's voice, even though he had found a way to fuse it with pity and compassion. "Throwing the old man in jail would do no one any good. He's not a physical threat to anyone, but by taking his pension away he's going to have to get another job or live like a pauper. Doing community service will make up for all those years he basically stole money from the county by not enforcing fines. I do feel sorry for him, even though I know he was responsible for his own choices. I have to wonder, if his wife wouldn't have needed that expensive medicine, would he have taken the same approach. I guess we have no right to judge him. We need to ask ourselves, put in his situation, what might we have done?" His gaze shifted from person to person waiting to see if anyone would respond to his assessment. The question brought a hushed silence to the room, but within minutes Uncle Don stood and faced everyone in the room. "Ya'll know I'm a straight shooter and I've lived in Corbin all my life. Sheriff Baxter has been a household name in these parts for over forty years. I remember his wife, Dottie. She was a good influence on Baxter and when she became ill, desperation took over his life. I'm not trying to excuse him for the things he did, but I don't think everybody should be so hard on him. I know he had many opportunities to change his ways and he didn't. Because of that, yes, he needs to be punished. Back in the day, desperation was real, and so were the Mafia. Standing up to them was almost impossible."

Uncle Don crossed his arms over his chest and looked directly at Max. "What your mother did, Max, was self-sacrificing and very gutsy. I know you're feeling some resentment toward her, but she did what she felt was the right thing. Holding a grudge against her won't help, but allowing yourself to feel grateful that we've found each other will provide you and Molly happiness for your future."

A tight note in Uncle Don's voice hinted at concern. "I hope you will remember the scripture, 'If any of you are without sin, let him be the first to throw the stone.' There are going to be a lot of stones cast around town in the next few months so I hope you all will be able to encourage people to forgive and forget."

Alice placed her hand on Don's forearm and proudly said, "You do have a way with words, dear!"

Everyone said their goodbyes and promised Uncle Don they would do their best.

Chapter 37

Max and Molly

Max and Molly drove to the park where he had first seen Molly so eloquently stuffing her mouth full of hot dog. He smiled at that memory as he spread a blanket on top of the picnic table and motioned for Molly to sit. He returned to the car for the bottle of wine and glasses.

Molly lay back on the blanket waiting for Max, and observing the sky. A quarter moon hung remotely in the distance, surrounded by limitless stars. She felt small, lying here under the cover of this huge world, especially knowing these were the same stars that had lit her path halfway around the world, in Afghanistan. The only difference now, no night sounds, such as bombing or gun fire could be heard. Tonight, the only sounds were the hoot of an owl echoing in the distance and the chirp of crickets. The night air was brisk but warm enough not to need a sweater.

Molly felt the solitude of her thoughts wash over her. She finally felt accepted in this world and able now to appreciate the sacredness and beauty of life. She had felt led to this part of the country to find peace and a simpler way of life. She had not only found the serenity she so desired, but she had found love. Romantic love with Max and an inspiring love for the people of Corbin.

It suddenly dawned on Molly what Dane's words had meant when he had cautioned her about the folks on the mountain. He had implied they had an unbendable faith in God. They could move mountains, he said, anywhere they wanted. She knew he had not meant that literally, but total understanding of that statement had not come to light until recently. She had witnessed the "hill folks" strong belief in God and initiated questions, just as Dane said she would. They welcomed her uncertainties with open arms and responded with simple, yet powerful answers. Nellie, the Doyene of the Mountain, had graciously given Molly a Bible and insisted she memorize some verses. The more she read, the more intrigued she became. She was sure now that her decision to come to Corbin had been inspired by God. Had He not spoken to her heart and had she not obeyed, her life could have taken a wrong turn.

Max returned with not only the wine, but cheese and crackers.

"You looked to be in some very serious thoughts, Molly. Are you alright?"

"I'm fine Max. I feel as though I've been searching for something all my life, never knowing what it was, but I think I've found it."

"And what is that?"

"Acceptance. I finally feel balance in my life, like this is where I'm meant to be."

Max sat down beside her on the blanket, leaned over and kissed her on the cheek. "You know, that's exactly how I feel too. I never seemed to belong anywhere until I moved here. With everything that's in my family history, it amazes me how I ended up here, in this tiny town. And the thing that really amazes me is the fact that you ended up here too."

The power in his gaze held her still. Molly's eyes brimmed with tears as she spoke. "When I think about how I got here, there's no doubt in my mind it was God. As much as I hate what happened to me in Afghanistan, none of this would have been possible without that incident. "

Max was studying her with an intense gaze.

"You don't understand do you, Max? Think about it. Because of Lieutenant Walker, I refused to park in the parking garage which meant you would never have rescued me if I hadn't walked by your building. Your heroic attempt to save me caused anxiety in my life which in turn gave me the push I needed to confide in my therapist about the night in Afghanistan. After my admission to what happened, I knew I needed a simpler life. That's when I answered the ad at Dane's clinic. If God hadn't set all of that in to motion, none of what I just talked about would have happened. He may have sent me on the scenic route, but because of this journey, I have had the chance to free myself from the guilt I was feeling. I realize Lieutenant Walker should have shouldered the entire burden of guilt. It was not my fault and I will not feel guilty anymore."

"I totally agree with you about everything. Think about my story and how I ended up in Corbin. Do you think God had a hand in that too?"

Molly's tight expression relaxed into a smile as her voice drifted into a hushed whisper. "As a nurse, I've stood at the side of many beds and I've heard many stories. A lot of them involved God. I would always listen and smile but in my heart, I never believed them. They were important to my patients so I made it look like I understood. But I didn't. I remember one of my patients, Mrs. Williams, tried to explain to me about God's timing. She said it wasn't like ours. She would hold my hand and tell me that God never makes mistakes and the answer we want is not always the answer we get, but the answer we get is always the right one, the one God has chosen. She said we may not understand it but we need to believe it. Do you think she was right?"

"I've never been a church-going guy but I have nothing against those who do. Would you like to find a church and try it out? My friend Mike, at work, goes every Sunday. I'll ask him if we could join him, if you want to."

"I would. I feel blessed to think that God has chosen this path for me. I wish I could have taken a shorter way to get here, but maybe my stubbornness had something to do with it. I'm wondering now just how many times God tried to get my attention and I just didn't hear Him."

Max smiled and gave her a wink. "I guess He knew you were really hungry the day I saw you shoving that hot dog into your mouth as if there was going to be no tomorrow."

Molly gave a short laugh filled with embarrassment. "I wanted to hurry up and finish the hot dog before you saw me. but it was too late."

"So, you had already seen me and you were trying to get away without speaking?"

"To be truthful, yes. I couldn't believe it was you. I thought you were stalking me."

Max lowered his head close to Molly and said, "My only focus that day was a piece of dough with sugar on top. You weren't even on my mind – until I saw red hair. Then I couldn't stop thinking about you."

Molly offered him a small, shy smile and said, "I'm glad we were both hungry that day. I think we should hang around on the path God has planned and see where it takes us. I'm honestly excited about my future. About our future."

Max agreed. "I'm willing to take the chance if you are."

Chapter 38

Family

Months passed and most people had forgotten about the trial. Sheriff Baxter could be seen many days during the month picking up trash along Route 21. Silas had bought a small house on the west side of town where he planned to spend the winter months with his new found family. The love letters had been delivered to him and many nights by his small fireplace, he read every page slowly, cherishing each word. Occasionally he would break down in tears as he imagined his life with Isabella and Max.

He had been asked to speak to small groups about his life and his decision to move back to Corbin, after such a long separation. He found the process to be helpful in rebuilding his self-esteem and baring his sincerity to the people of Corbin. The words from his heart had also brought healing to his soul.

Silas and Max spent many hours together and formed a great relationship. Isabella's true reasons for the separation from the family were never uncovered. Silas shamelessly admitted his pride had been outwardly directed towards Isabella in a foolish and corrupt way. Wearing a uniform and serving in the US Navy had given him a much more favorable view of himself than the mirror revealed. When Isabella quit communicating with him, he allowed that arrogant assumption of superiority to blind himself with the attitude he would not beg for her love.

In hindsight, Silas wished the past twenty-eight years could have been spent with Isabella but regret was something he had to live with, a pain caused by deep disappointment. He had enabled that hurt to grow into anger. As he grew older, that corrosive emotion evaporated slowly and faded into what he now realized was a form of grief. Grief, compounded by feelings of guilt and confusion over losing Isabella.

Even though Silas had been eaten up by regret, pride and loneliness, he could now put all that behind him and enjoy his time with his family. He devoted his spare time to Max and Molly, supportive of their love for each other and for the community.

Max surprised Molly with a proposal, planning the wedding for the spring. The entire town was invited, specifying a symbolic time of renewal for all its residents.

Silas campaigned for the next election and became Sheriff of Boone County for the next four years. Diggor continued to serve as Deputy until he died of a heart attack while helping Sheriff Baxter pick up trash along the road.

A new sign was proudly erected, welcoming visitors to Corbin, Home of Kentucky Fried Chicken and the Moonbow. Max and Molly Callahan, because of their care and commitment to the folks of Boone County, became legendary. The Callahan Clinic was built in their honor by an anonymous donor, giving the residents an up-to-date health center.

The conspiracies and political secrets that had plagued the town for so long had been put to rest, thanks to Max's novice detective work. His father, Silas had brought new life to the town after being elected Sheriff.

Molly launched a new program at the clinic for women in offensive situations or victims of sexual abuse. Memories of her own ordeal gave her the empathy she needed to help these women. Aunt Alice volunteered her time and wisdom to those who needed help sharing their dark secrets. She helped them understand that keeping a secret may be clever, but having no secrets to keep is even wiser.

Observe with sparkling eyes the entire world around you because the ultimate secrets are forever hidden in the most incredible places.

www.ingramcontent.com/pod-product-compliance
Lightning Source LLC
Chambersburg PA
CBHW021948290426
44108CB00012B/989